DREAMS AND
GUIDED IMAGERY

DREAMS AND GUIDED IMAGERY

Gifts for Transforming Illness and Crisis

Tallulah Lyons, M.Ed.

BALBOA.
PRESS
A DIVISION OF HAY HOUSE

ISBN: 978-1-4525-5026-8 (sc)
ISBN: 978-1-4525-5025-1 (e)

Balboa Press books may be ordered through booksellers or by contacting:

Balboa Press
A Division of Hay House
1663 Liberty Drive
Bloomington, IN 47403
www.balboapress.com
1-(877) 407-4847

Because of the dynamic nature of the Internet, any web addresses or links contained in this book may have changed since publication and may no longer be valid. The views expressed in this work are solely those of the author and do not necessarily reflect the views of the publisher, and the publisher hereby disclaims any responsibility for them.

The author of this book does not dispense medical advice or prescribe the use of any technique as a form of treatment for physical, emotional, or medical problems without the advice of a physician, either directly or indirectly. The intent of the author is only to offer information of a general nature to help you in your quest for emotional and spiritual well-being. In the event you use any of the information in this book for yourself, which is your constitutional right, the author and the publisher assume no responsibility for your actions.

Any people depicted in stock imagery provided by Thinkstock are models, and such images are being used for illustrative purposes only.
Certain stock imagery © Thinkstock.

Printed in the United States of America

Balboa Press rev. date: 5/09/2012

PRAISE FOR DREAMS AND GUIDED IMAGERY

"Tallulah Lyons offers a comprehensible guide to dream imagery, demonstrating the important role it plays in integrative medicine. By including scripts, worksheets, and exercises, she offers tools to support the work that health care professionals and volunteers are called to do. Tallulah uses her years of experience to give noteworthy examples of the dreams, the revelations, and the healing that come to those who are part of a health centered dream group. I highly recommend *Dreams and Guided Imagery* to enhance the power of dreams in healing our bodies, spirits, and souls."

———JUSTINA LASLEY, Founder and Director
of Institute for Dream Studies and author of *Honoring the Dream:
A Handbook for Dream Group Leaders*

"In *Dreams and Guided Imagery*, Tallulah Lyons provides a path for readers to mine the rich fields of dream work in order to actively engage their unconscious inner resources. This important work is a vital aspect of an integrative approach to medicine which includes looking at all levels of our being and experience. I highly recommend this book to anyone seeking a tool to interact with dreams and guided imagery as a part of a life practice centered on embracing health and wholeness."

———MATTHEW P. MUMBER, M.D.,
Harbin Clinic Radiation Oncology Center,
editor of *Integrative Oncology: Principles and Practice*

"*Dreams and Guided Imagery* is packed with practical guides for transforming the nightmares and fears typical of people facing a physical crisis. The scripts for guided relaxation and visualizations are especially effective. Lyons invites readers to join the Dream Circle as each member learns, through his or her personal symbolic images, how to grow toward a more expansive and satisfying life. Readers gain insight along with members of the circle. Even experienced dream workers will find valuable tools for transforming fear in themselves and their clients into life-enhancing growth. I'm glad to recommend this practical and inspiring book!"

———PATRICIA GARFIELD, author of *Creative Dreaming,*
Healing Power of Dreams, etc.,
Co-founder and past president of IASD

"This is benchmark, not only for the field of dream work with cancer patients, but for the field of dream work as a whole. The reader will find many poignant and carefully documented examples and tested techniques and suggestions about how to bring forth healing energies and possibilities– even from the worst nightmares. Written with the quiet authority of experience and unobtrusive elegance of a gifted writer, this book will be of use and profound interest to the absolute beginner and the seasoned expert alike."

———THE REVEREND JEREMY TAYLOR, D. MIN.,
author of *The Wisdom of Your Dreams*, etc., Co-founder and Past President of IASD, Founder-Director of the Marin Institute for Projective Dream Work (MIPD), Member of the Board of the Unitarian Universalist Society for Community Ministry (UUSCM)

"Tallulah Lyons is on the cutting edge of dreams and healing. Wisdom gained from her own experience and her work with groups and individuals opens up the possibility for the reader to discover messages from dreams about their own health and healing. Reading this book will introduce and immerse you into that world."

——THE REVEREND ROBERT L. HADEN, JR.,
Director of The Haden Institute and author of *Unopened Letters From God: Using Biblical Dreams to Unlock Your Nightly Dreams*

"This book not only provides a wealth of techniques for receiving guidance from your dreams but also serves as an in-depth handbook for healing and care-giving practitioners. It is filled with case studies that envelop the reader in beautiful real-life stories of how dreams can guide us through both the emotional and physical healing processes in times of need."

—ROBERT HOSS, author and Director with IASD
and the DreamScience Foundation

"I know from my many years of research on dreams and from my clinical experience, that dreams are the most connective and creative parts of our minds. Dreams sometimes pick up hints about physical illness, and also emotional problems of which we are not aware in our waking lives; and dreams can help us be more in touch with ourselves. *Dreams and Guided Imagery* is an excellent and well-written book based on years of work with cancer patients sharing dreams in a group setting. It is full of vivid examples, as well as suggestions and instructions for the reader. I recommend it highly, not only for patients with cancer, but for anyone who wants to learn from dreams in a group setting."

——ERNEST HARTMANN, M.D.,
first Editor-in-Chief of the journal Dreaming,
and author of twelve books, most recently,
The Nature and Function of Dreaming and Boundaries: A New Way to Look at the World

CONTENTS

Disclaimer

This book is not intended to replace or to be a substitute for appropriate medical care or psychological counseling. The practices of dream appreciation and guided imagery as put forth in this book are intended to be used as complements to conventional medical care. Dreams speak the language of symbol and metaphor. Please avoid literal interpretation, particularly with dreams about disaster and disease. Unexpected issues and emotions may arise when practicing dream appreciation or guided imagery. Please seek professional health care for individual concerns. The author assumes no responsibility or liability for the actions of the reader.

Acknowledgements

I want to express my deepest gratitude to so many people who have helped bring this book to fruition. To Wendy Pannier, my co-creator in the Cancer Project, and all the project facilitators who have worked with us and shared our passion. To the International Association for the Study of Dreams (IASD) and its support for our work. To the hundreds of participants who have attended our workshops, and to the dreamers in ongoing groups whose stories and dreams, though altered to protect individuals, make up the foundation of this book.

To Mariane Schaum, my dear friend and inspiring editor whose constant encouragement and editing skills have brought this book to life.

To Carolyn Helmer, Manager of Cancer Wellness at Piedmont Hospital, for her faith in dreams and healing imagery and her encouraging support of my passion through the years. To Rachel Newby, Program Director at Cancer Support Community at Northside Hospital, for her enthusiastic support through the years. To my friends and colleagues at Cancer Wellness and Cancer Support Community. To the directors of cancer centers across the country who have invited our workshops. To all the participants through the years in the Monday guided imagery group and the Tuesday dream circle.

To my teacher, analyst, and friend, Jerry Wright. To my mentors, Jeremy Taylor, Bob Haden, Robert Hoss, and all the faculty of the Haden Institute. To my models for guided imagery, Belleruth Naparstek and Martin Rossman. To my models in integrative medicine, Rachel Naomi Remen, and Michael Lerner. To authors and workshop teachers at the beginning of my journey, Justina Lasley, Robert Johnson, John Sanford, Marion Woodman, and Jean Shinoda Bolen. To authors and workshop teachers who inspire my journey now, especially James Hollis and Jutta von Buchholtz. To authors of my favorite dream books, Jeremy Taylor, Patricia Garfield, Montague Ullman, Ernest Hartmann, Robert Hoss, Kelly Bulkeley, Alan Siegel, Justina Lasley, David Gordon, and Marc Barasch.

To Carl Jung and his gift of *Memories, Dreams, Reflections*. To integrative medicine researchers in the fields of dreams and guided imagery.

To all who read parts of the manuscript and helped it to evolve— especially Rachel Norment and Owen Norment. Also Wendy Pannier, Linda McCabe, Zoe Newman, Rachelle Oppenhuizen, Helene Rhodes, Nancy Yingst, Betsy McCabe, Nancy Land, Ave Collins, Jackie Lawrence, Laura Hileman, and Diane Rooks. To many others who have provided constant support, especially Betty Lingo, Vicki Woodyard, Sue Anthony, Sheila Asato, Ryan Hurd, the "Justina" dream group, and the Sunday dream group. Special thanks to Lisa South for her creative work on cover image; and to Dory Codington for help with the quilt square.

My deepest gratitude to each member of my family. My hope is that as you have supported my dreams, so too will you always support your own. To Betsy and Loch, David and Maria, thank you. To William, Oliver, Clarissa, Eric, and Hannah, thank you. Wherever they take you, may your dreams bless you.

And especially to Bill, thank you for your love that has sustained and inspired me through the years and for your companionship on this continuing journey.

FOREWORD

Dream literature abounds with accounts of dreams and healing, from the Yellow Emperor's Book on Internal Medicine written thousands of years ago to the dream temples of Asclepius to current research on psychoneuroimmunology. Physicians from Hippocrates to Bernie Siegel have found that dreams can often predict illness before the symptoms become obvious and readily diagnosable. I am co-founder with Tallulah Lyons of the Cancer Project of the International Association for the Study of Dreams (IASD). Our passion is to bring understanding of the healing gifts of dreams into the field of integrative medicine. Our work demonstrates how dreams can serve as powerful allies during any encounter with crisis and disease.

I came to this understanding through first-hand experience as I used dreams to help me survive late-stage cancer. In June 1993 I had a dream that was trying to convey to me that I had a serious estrogen imbalance, but I did not understand the meaning at the time. About four months later, I had a vivid dream, the kind I have come to realize is often precognitive. In the dream my gynecologist called me and said, "Wendy, you need to have a D&C." That was the entirety of the dream. I told my gynecologist about the excessively heavy bleeding and cramping I was having every month, but it was dismissed as probable fibroids. When the problems persisted and worsened, I was sent for a sonogram. A few days later my gynecologist called—for the first time in the 20 years I had been seeing her—and said, "Wendy, you need to have a D&C."

In early January 1995, the results of the D&C showed that I had endometrial cancer, also known as uterine cancer. A hysterectomy shortly thereafter showed that the cancer had metastasized; my condition was categorized as Stage IVB. This cancer, like ovarian cancer, is not detected by a pap test. But my dreams had been warning me of the problem for 18 months.

Throughout my treatment, dreams were my allies. Some were nightmarish while others were encouraging. Shortly before diagnosis, I dreamed that a building I owned was imploding and that it would take six months to rebuild. My body—my "building"—*was* imploding with the cancer; the experimental protocol I was prescribed would take about six months. Later I had a dream about renovating a building I owned from the basement up. I awoke from this dream feeling very positive. When I meditated with the dream, it gave me hope and helped me through some difficult chemotherapy sessions.

I kept track of all my dreams, and found correspondence between the evolving imagery and how I was working through emotional as well as physical issues. Dreams warned me when I developed blood clots and reassured me—at a time of great sadness midway through treatment—that my destination was only three miles (months) away. My dream imagery amazed me. It used metaphors that spoke a language that resonated with my life experiences. Working with dreams during my cancer experience taught me that I could access powerful energy by using the imagery from my own dreams in self-guided imagery sessions.

Upon going into remission in the fall of 1995, I began conducting workshops on dream work with people facing cancer. I used my own recent experiences plus years of training in dream work prior to the cancer. I met Tallulah Lyons at an IASD conference in 2000. In the early 1990s she had been a dream-sharing companion to a life-long friend who was dying from cancer. This inspired her to create a dream group for other cancer patients. We immediately recognized the similarities in our work, and became friends and colleagues.

Our training and group dream work approaches were similar. I had extensive experience with Dr. Montague Ullman while Tallulah had worked with Jeremy Taylor and studied at the Haden Institute. We were both conducting workshops and ongoing groups in cancer support centers. We recognized that integrating the personalized imagery of dreams could greatly enhance the healing potential of well-researched mind/body practices already offered in many cancer facilities, such as guided imagery, meditation, yoga, and the expressive arts.

In 2003 we decided to join forces and seek grant funding. We worked through IASD's Development Committee and submitted a grant proposal through IASD. It was turned down. Disappointed but undaunted, we spent the next year addressing areas the foundation had seen as weaknesses in our proposal. We kept careful track of our accomplishments and in 2004 submitted proposals to two foundations. We received small grants from each.

During 2005 those grants enabled us to formalize what we had been doing for years. First, we created a manual for participants in our workshops and ongoing groups entitled *The Healing Power of Dreams and Nightmares*. Intended as a resource, it covers everything from the history of dreams and healing to frequently asked questions about dreams and nightmares, tips for recalling and recording dreams, and symbol work. It also provides techniques for working with dreams, emphasizing the use of dream images in guided imagery exercises. The final sections of the manual cover ways to honor dreams and instructions on working with dreams at home; they also include various worksheets and other resources.

Next, we developed a *Facilitator's Manual* that contains a discussion of key issues in working with people facing cancer, suggestions for how to work with healing dream imagery and nightmare imagery, outlines for workshops and ongoing groups, and instructions on the use of the evaluation and assessment tools we designed. Based on our accomplishments with the initial grants, we were awarded additional small grants from both foundations the following year. We then selected a small group of interested IASD members and used the grant money to train and supervise them as facilitators.

One of the ways we evaluate our work is to keep detailed records of the progression of positive imagery and evolving nightmare imagery for each member of our ongoing dream groups. We incorporated these outcome assessments into our grant reports and have continued to track them. The evolution and transformation of nightmare imagery, as shared in this book, demonstrate the powerful possibilities of ongoing dream work.

In the Cancer Project, we also use a quality of life survey. Each year since 2005, dream group participants have reported:

- They now use positive imagery from dreams in meditative activities.

- Their dream work brings about decreased feelings of anxiety and stress.

- They experience an increased sense of connection with others, an increased sense of connection to inner resources, an increased understanding of healing at multiple levels and an increased quality of life—particularly emotional, social and spiritual.

- They enjoy increased feelings of control over life and health issues, increased feelings of hope, and an increased understanding of how to live fully now, despite cancer.

Over the past few years, IASD facilitators and we have conducted workshops and ongoing dream groups in cancer facilities in over a dozen states. We always encourage the participants to evoke their healing dream imagery in other stress-reduction activities available at the cancer centers: guided imagery, journaling, art, expressive writing, yoga, tai chi, meditation, music. We also encourage participants to use their dream imagery during doctor visits, chemotherapy and radiation treatments, thus integrating the supportive energy from their dreams into all aspects of the healing process.

From our own profound experiences with dreams, from watching the healing transformation that occurs in dream group members over time, and from seeing research that attests to the importance of support groups, meditative activities, and imagery in the healing process, Tallulah and I firmly believe it is time for dream appreciation to be recognized as an important practice in integrative medicine. Our hope is to expand the IASD Cancer Project; to increase the number of facilitators; to increase the number of workshops and dream groups. We hope to inspire dream researchers to conduct studies with cancer patients and people with critical illness. With the publication of *Dreams and Guided Imagery*, we hope to expand the understanding of dreams and guided imagery as gifts for healing and living life to the fullest.

--Wendy Pannier

Wendy Pannier is a past president of the International Association for the Study of Dreams (IASD). She is co-creator with Tallulah Lyons of the IASD Cancer Project and author of numerous articles about dreaming. She frequently gives talks about her work, and is available for presentations and workshops.

1

CALLED TO THE JOURNEY

The healing journey usually begins with crisis: critical illness, divorce, the death of a loved one, financial ruin, an accident, natural disaster. A crisis turns life upside down and slams the door on habitual solutions. Crisis dictates stepping into the unknown and finding a new way.

The Chinese symbol for crisis is made up of two characters, one meaning *danger* and the other meaning *opportunity*. This ancient symbol implies that crises hold seeds for new possibility. One of the most exciting ways to explore the myriad possible pathways through crisis is to build an ongoing relationship with your dreams. Dreams (and the world of imagery) are filled with energy for healing.

Dreams usually intensify during crises. When one is diagnosed with serious illness, dreams may come in great floods. Many are nightmares filled with destruction and chaos. A nightmare is a loud call to let go of old ways, to move onto an uncharted path, to commit to an unpredictable direction. A crisis dream is a call to wake up to a larger relationship with life and to move beyond limiting attitudes, perceptions, and beliefs.

Just before and after diagnosis, nightmares about personal traumas from the past often increase. When dreamers explore these nightmares, they may become conscious of strengths and resources that once helped at a critical time. Given careful attention, such dreams can serve as a reminders and sources of strengths that are still available for the current illness. A crisis dream can become an invitation to find an expanded sense of meaning and unimaginable resources for healing.

Dreams speak in a symbolic and metaphoric language of imagery—emotionally laden, non-verbal stimuli that affect all the senses. When crisis strikes, like first responders, images from the inner world mobilize in the depths of the psyche and begin to push their way into consciousness in order to help. Like outer clothing, images provide perceivable forms for invisible dynamics. Dreams broadcast the specific imagery and energies that are needed for healing and expanded living.

HEALING VS CURING

Before talking about the healing nature of dreams, it is important to distinguish between the concepts of healing and curing. These concepts are often confused.

The word *curing* is used in the medical world to refer to the eradication of a particular disease. Usually curing is performed by someone or something outside your efforts and restores you to a previously existing state of health.

Healing, on the other hand, refers to a much broader concept. The word *healing* comes from the same source as the word *whole*. Therefore, "to heal" is synonymous with "to make whole." Healing is a process that takes place from the inside out. It addresses the causes and factors that are contributing to the disease; it focuses on the whole person with the intent of nourishing mind, body, and spirit. Even if you are not cured, healing brings you into a sense of balance and wholeness. It allows you to live fully, no matter the circumstances.

Sometimes the experiences of curing and healing overlap, but not always. In the field of integrative medicine, the goal is to offer a combination of complementary practices along with the best of conventional medical care in order to bring about a sense of healing to everyone who seeks a cure.

DIALOGUE WITH YOUR DREAMS

Dreams invite interaction and dialogue. What is the dialogue about? It is about forming an ever-expanding relationship with a source of support and creative wisdom. It is about living fully in each moment—moving away from fear and despair into a sense of healing and wholeness. Dream dialogue is about growing into your fullest potential through transforming places in your life where you are off base, stuck, or out of balance. It is about finding your special destiny and about finding direction and support for following your unique path.

In *Dreams and Guided Imagery: Gifts for Transforming Illness and Crisis*, you will learn dream appreciation and guided imagery techniques developed in the International Association for the Study of Dreams (IASD) Cancer Project. Approaches in this book are modeled by six patients who meet each week in a cancer support community to share dreams. The characters are drawn from actual participants in ongoing dream circles—more than one hundred fifty individuals whose dreams have helped them navigate the journey through cancer.

Although the participants have given permission to share their dreams and stories, the characters in the book, their dreams, and their quotations have been altered to protect the privacy of actual people. The essence of typical dreams and the dreamers' responses have been preserved, revealing a multifaceted, multilayered process of healing and growth witnessed through the years. We in the IASD Cancer Project hope that their stories and dreams will give you a sense of what it is like to be part of a dream circle.

We also hope that this book will inspire you to develop a dialogue with your own dreams, to enter the landscape of your own inner being, and allow the relationship to this deep realm of consciousness to help you grow and heal so that you can claim the fullness of your own creative spirit and the richness of expanded living no matter your present circumstances.

In *Dreams and Guided Imagery:*

- You will learn about patterns of thought, emotion and behavior that promote health and wholeness and about patterns that inhibit the process of living fully.

- You will discover how dreams bring imagery and energy to help you transform debilitating patterns into imagery and energy for healing.

- You will be shown how to breathe and relax into a deep meditative state.

- You will learn how to re-enter your dreams and the dreams of others through guided imagery so that you can participate in the transformation of nightmares and waking-world conflicts.

- You will discover ways to appreciate and dialogue with symbols from both dreams and waking life.

- You will learn how to evoke "waking dreams," guided imagery experiences that bring imagery and energies for creative living in response to conscious seeking.

- You will learn how to embody the energies of healing imagery and how to integrate the energies into the healing process and all aspects of your waking life.

MEETING THE DREAM CIRCLE

Laura facilitates the Dream Circle. She is a ten-year breast cancer survivor. Throughout and after treatment, she has pursued the study of several integrative practices including dream work, guided imagery, mindfulness meditation, yoga, and the therapeutic use of writing and art.

Recently diagnosed with breast cancer, **Amy**, a thirty-four year old Japanese-American, is the newest member of the group. She feels unsupported by her husband who travels and is rarely home, and by her mother who is an unrelenting critic. She worries about her eight-year-old son. Amy is an artist and had been interviewing for a job in a gallery when she was diagnosed. She is heart-broken over having to withdraw her name from the application process because of her treatment for cancer. She is frightened and frustrated.

Jay, a construction worker, has a wife and two children. After being diagnosed with early-stage thyroid cancer, he had surgery last month to remove most of his thyroid gland. Jay obsesses over the slight possibility that the surgery will affect his voice. He worries about his job and financial security for his family.

In her early sixties, **Margaret** has completed chemotherapy for ovarian cancer. Her hair, which was straight before she lost it in treatment, has come back in lovely thick, silver-white waves. Margaret is a quilter and works on her newest quilt during Dream Circle meetings. Her husband is a recovering alcoholic. They have grown children and a new grandbaby.

Thirty-five-year-old **Emily** completed treatment for cervical cancer a year ago. She is back at work, but arranges time to come to the dream circle. Now she is caught up in a crisis with Andrew, her partner of five years, who is in turmoil about their future together.

Sam, a recently divorced, forty-five-year-old African American, is in treatment for prostate cancer. Early each morning he has radiation treatment. Sam is a social worker and continues to see clients at a local mental health center. He has worked with his dreams for many years and often helps clients explore their dreams.

In her seventies, **Rachel** is the oldest member of the Dream Circle. Every day she covers her head with a turban or hat because she lost her hair in chemotherapy treatment. Though she thrives on the support of the group and almost never misses a session, she is a very concrete, rational thinker and has difficulty with the meditative, intuitive, and symbolic approaches she experiences in the dream circle. She struggles to see beyond literal understanding. She is in treatment for non-Hodgkin's lymphoma, and is presently doing well.

DREAM CIRCLE MEETING

The group gathers in a cozy meeting room with overstuffed chairs circled about a low coffee table. Laura lights a candle in the center, and after introductions and brief check-in time, she leads the group in a guided imagery journey into the liminal space of dream dialogue.

MODEL SCRIPT FOR OPENING MEDITATION

What follows is an example of an opening guided meditation that helps members of the circle shift from the swirling thoughts and emotions they come in with into a quiet and centered level of consciousness. This script is simply a model. When you read a script in this book, read slowly. Allow yourself to hear and feel the words. Allow yourself to sink into the liminal space of meditative consciousness even as you read.

> Getting as comfortable as you can . . . closing your
> eyes if you like . . . sinking into the support of the
> chair or couch . . . beginning to take several deep,
> relaxing breaths . . . breathing in through your
> nose the warm energy of renewal . . . and with each
> out breath, breathing out whatever needs to be let
> go. Inhaling, renewing . . . exhaling, releasing . . .
> focusing on breath moving in . . . breath moving
> out . . . expanding all the way up from your abdomen
> with the in-breath . . . slowly softening with the
> out-breath . . . feeling the flow of renewing energy
> moving throughout your body . . . and with each

breath, imagine moving down, down . . . deeper and
deeper toward a centered place within . . . moving
down on the waves of the breath to the centered core
of your being . . .

Now scanning your body . . . checking in to see
where you might be holding tension . . . carefully
scanning . . . and sending the warm energy of
the breath into any place that might need special
tending . . . allowing the warm breath to penetrate
any place that needs care . . . warming . . .
softening . . . relaxing . . . renewing . . .

Imagining a flow of life energy inside your body . . .
perhaps flowing as streams of light, perhaps as
streams of color, perhaps feeling vibration . . . a free
flow of life energy moving unimpeded throughout
your body from your toes to your head, from your
head to your toes and throughout your limbs . . .
unimpeded life energy now nourishing every organ,
every tissue, every tiny cell . . . and as all your body's
systems relax and harmonize . . . shifting your
attention . . .

And now imagining yourself standing at the rim
of a beautiful wellspring where inner resources
bubble up as offerings to fill your extended cup . . .
watching the flow . . . listening to the sounds . . .
feeling the air on your skin . . . opening your heart
to this wellspring of unending possibilities bubbling
up before you . . . extending your cup to the clear
flow of creative inspiration . . . extending to the
flow of intuitive wisdom . . . dipping into the
shining streams of imagery and energies that come
to invite you to new possibilities . . . opening to the
wellspring . . . filling your cup . . .

Opening all your senses . . . opening your
emotions . . . now opening your heart to reconnect
with your dream, whatever dream or dream-like

experience has come to be shared with the group today . . . gathering in all the details of your experience . . . allowing the dream to become a vivid, present reality . . .

Now slowly returning to our circle . . . grounded in your own deep center . . . ready to dialogue with the mysteries, the new possibilities of the dreams that have come to be shared.[1]

DREAM GATHERING

Restful peace, yet enlivened anticipation permeates the room. One by one, members of the Dream Circle quietly read or tell their dreams. They have written them in dream journals, in the present tense, so that as they share, they are once again caught up in the immediacy of the experience. They have each given their dream a title that helps catch the essence of the dream. Before reading the dream, the dreamer reads the title and names the primary feelings evoked by the dream.

Today, Amy, the newest member of the circle, is the last to speak, but she has brought a dream for the first time. Through tears, she says, "I used to love my dreams. When I was a little girl I had some fabulous dreams! I could even fly! But since my diagnosis, my dreams are nightmares. Right now I hate my dreams. In them I'm chased by shadowy men or keep losing my way. In this latest dream I try to buy a ticket to get home and end up with a ticket to some place else. The ticket seller man is frightening!"

Laura asks, "Have you given the dream a title?"

"No," Amy replies. "I guess I'll call it *Ticket to Some Place Else.*"

"What feelings do you experience in the dream?" Laura asks.

Amy sighs deeply and says, "I feel angry and afraid."

Laura says, "Would you be willing to share this dream? Your dream is unique, but I'll bet everyone in this room has had some version of it and has felt aspects of the fear and anger."

Amy nods, and Laura continues. "Just close your eyes, breathe, relax, drop back down into your center and reconnect with your dream. Open all your senses. Allow the experience to become real. Read or tell us the dream like it's happening right now. The rest of us will listen with our eyes closed and imagine that we are the one who is experiencing the dream. We'll feel the emotions as our own. We'll allow the dream to stir up our own stuff. When we respond, we'll share our own feelings about how the dream touches us personally, our feelings about our own experience. So if you'll now reconnect with the dream; and when you are ready, read or tell us the dream."[2]

Dream Circle members close their eyes, and after a short silence, Amy begins to read her dream, *Ticket to Some Place Else.*

> "I'm in a small airport—not one I ever really saw—but I think it's in a hot, tropical place. Yes, there are lots of native-looking people with bright colorful clothes. I know I need to get home. Yes, I want to go home and I don't have a ticket. I go up to the counter. The ticket seller is a small, shriveled up little guy with no teeth and he gives me a sinister look. He doesn't listen when I tell him where I need to go. He just writes a ticket, takes my money and shoves the ticket at me. The whole time, he's giving me mean looks and kind of laughing under his breath like something is very funny.
>
> "Now, I'm walking away and when I look down, I see the ticket is for somewhere I've never heard of. I turn back to the counter. The ugly guy is smirking at me, and then it hits me that the rest of the airport is completely empty. All the people have disappeared. I feel terrified and totally alone. Then I wake up."

Amy's tears rise to the surface and she pulls out more tissue.

Laura speaks. "Please, let us hear the dream one more time. Try to be fully present in the dream. All of us will be imagining that this is our own dream and we'll be opening to feel all the emotions. Please let us hear the dream one more time."

Quieting her tears and, rather than reading the dream, Amy keeps her eyes closed and repeats the dream slowly. She pauses several times as the dream becomes an emotionally-charged reality. At the end of the telling, Amy is calm.

"Thank you, Amy," Laura says. "Each of us is now feeling the dream as our own. Now we'll ask you a few questions so that our own version of the dream is clear.[3] Remember, you are always in charge of this questioning process. You have total choice in how or whether you respond to any question."[4]

Amy nods. "Okay, I'm ready."

CLARIFYING QUESTIONS

Sam begins. "Amy, you say it's a small airport in a hot, tropical place. Can you tell us more about this airport?"

"I've actually never been to any airport like it. But in the dream, I see native people in colorful clothes and it is hot with fans and no air conditioning . . . Oh my God! My husband travels all the time. He goes down to the Bahamas on business at least once a month. He's always gone. Do you guess this is why this place is in my dream? I hate it that he's gone all the time!"

Laura steers Amy back to Sam's question. "Tell us more about the natives in colorful clothes."

Amy tries to focus. "Several cute little kids are running around playing. A mother in a bright teal dress holds a sleeping baby. Lots of bright, primary colors. A spunky old lady in a red dress is wearing a big hat covered with fruit. All these people seem happy, talking, laughing. Each person has several cloth sacks. It's their luggage. Piles of multi-colored sacks."

Emily speaks softly. "Tell us again everything you can about the ticket seller."

Amy keeps her eyes closed. "He's small . . . ugly . . . sinister . . . weird . . . no teeth . . . mean . . . probably enjoys tricking people . . . scary . . . doesn't listen . . . I know he likes his power . . . likes writing a ticket I don't want."

Jay continues questioning. "What is the destination written on the ticket in your hand?"

Amy says, "I have no idea. I can't read the name. But it isn't what I paid for. It's a ticket to somewhere else."

Laura asks the group, "Are there any more clarifying questions?"

Rachel chimes in. "Yes. Tell us more about the stuffed sacks."

Amy frowns and re-imagines the sacks. She looks puzzled. "I think they hold mostly gifts for the people these passengers are going to visit. And clothes for being on vacation, probably."

Laura asks again, "More questions? . . . No?"

Then she addresses Amy. "Amy, at one point you mentioned the Bahamas where your husband frequently travels. Maybe you noticed that instead of pursuing that association, I steered you back to elaborating on the imagery of the dream. When we are in a group, we try to keep the dream itself in sharp focus and not discuss the dreamer's personal associations until the group has had a chance to project onto the dream. When each person has talked about the dream as if it is his or her dream, then it is the dreamer's turn to offer personal associations and insights to the extent that he or she wants to share."

Laura looks around the group. "If there are no more clarifying questions, then let's move to the next part of our process."

SHARING PROJECTIONS

"We call this the 'If it were my dream' or 'In my dream' time," Laura says. "Each person has listened to your dream, has felt the emotions, and is now ready to offer some reflections as if it is his or her very own dream. This is called a projective dream-work approach.[5] Each person who responds will be projecting personal experiences, perceptions, attitudes and emotions onto your dream. The group members are not trying to 'interpret' your dream for you, but it is very likely that their personal projections will bring you some insight. Right now, you can simply listen to the reflections and notice if you resonate with anything being said. If you look down and take notes while you're listening, the group will be reminded that they are sharing with one another and are not 'interpreting' for you. After the discussion, then it will be your turn again to respond."

Rachel speaks first as she folds her empty lunch sack. "This dream really stirs me up. It's a dream that in many ways is indeed my dream. When I was first diagnosed with non-Hodgkin's lymphoma, it was exactly as if I had been sold a ticket to some place I absolutely did not want to go. In my dream, I'm imagining the ticket seller as a sinister force that seems to just grab control of my life. Back when I was diagnosed, my life felt like it was in the hands of a diabolical trickster. Still does some of the time. I go in and out of anger and feeling victimized."

Emily responds next. "In my dream, I'm really struck by the fact that this guy has no teeth. I see him as pretty old and feeble, and therefore he can't bite me. I feel he's unhealthy and isn't going to have a lot of strength to hurt me for much longer. For me, he's kind of a comic book monster who symbolizes my old habitual reactions of fear and doom whenever I faced an unknown situation. I used to dream a lot about ugly little guys who were out to get me. I think they were images that came to challenge my diminished self-image. But I've worked hard to try to deal with scary situations as if they're challenges and opportunities. Like my cancer. Turning fear into opportunity isn't easy, but now, some of the tough guys who show up in my dreams have become helpful. I think of these recent guys as symbols of my growing sense of strength, trust, and hope. These guys are resources that are deep inside me. This ticket seller with no teeth—for me, he's an old fearful, reactive part of me who hopefully I can transform into an ally."

Margaret says, "And in my dream, I'm focusing on the native people in their colorful clothes. They sound like an artful symbol of life and hope. For me, bright colors always symbolize positive energy. The teal dress stands out for me. Teal is a color I associate with healing."

She displays her turquoise ring. "I wear a lot of teal and turquoise. And I love the image of the old woman in the red dress and fruity hat. She feels like a counterbalance to the weird ticket seller man. It feels like the dream is inviting me to focus on my *native* knowing, my basic instinctual wisdom, and to focus on my child-like energies symbolized by those kids running around in the airport. I think the dream wants me to tune into the energy of the mother with the new baby, for me, a symbol of new possibilities. The dream is inviting me to trust all this colorful positive energy that is somewhere deep inside me. This will help balance my fear of my ticket to who knows where."

Jay's reply is barely audible. "If this is my dream, I'm realizing it's trying to connect me with how lonely I feel with my spouse. It's connecting me with how alone and unsupported I feel. For me, when a dream connects me to strong emotions, then there are usually some new possibilities for dealing with them that I haven't considered yet. I'll try to work on how I feel about my relationship with my spouse, and . . . I'll look for a new way to communicate my feelings."

Sam is the last to speak. "In my dream, I'm reminded that I want to go home. Home is a huge symbol for me. For me, home is wherever I feel I'm totally connected . . . It's hard for me to feel at home anywhere. I feel this dream has come to help me see how connected I am to everybody in this group. Every one of us has felt at some time that we're holding a ticket to some place we didn't choose to go. Every one of us has felt loss of control and that we're suddenly alone. Amy, we hope you now know you're in good company and that you're not alone."

BACK TO THE DREAMER

Laura asks Amy. "Would you like to respond to any of the reflections?"

The room is quiet. Amy looks at each member of the circle and sighs. "What can I say? The dream was such a nightmare. But listening to your responses it no longer feels so grim . . . I get the feeling that all of you are looking at the dream as a source of help. You're seeing the elements of the dream as symbols . . . like the ticket seller as a symbol of my fear . . . like the bright people as symbols of hope and having fun. I think I kind of get it. You're giving me a lot to think about.

BASICS FOR YOU, THE READER, TO THINK ABOUT

As you begin to explore your own dreams, keep these assumptions in mind:

- Every dream brings imagery and energies that can help you expand relationship with your deepest self, with others, and with the creative energies of the dream.

- Interacting with dreams over time can deepen your relationship with a powerful source of wisdom and restorative energy.

- Every dream, including the worst nightmare, can be a path to greater health and wholeness.

- Dreams point to where you are stuck and blocked and also stir up your heart's deepest yearnings, helping you find a sense of meaningful direction.

- The imagery of dreams is composed primarily of emotionally-laden symbols and metaphors.

- Symbols contain multiple meanings all at one time and offer potential for healing and growth on multiple levels of mind, body, emotion, and spirit, all at the same time.

- Dream exploration is most fruitful when the dreamer responds to the dream from a deep meditative level of consciousness. Guided imagery is a practice that can immerse the dreamer in a transformative space between consciousness and unconsciousness. In this creative, meditative space, rational and verbal processing can dialogue with intuitive and sensate processing, compounding the wisdom of both.

- Dreams and nightmares can be transformed through guided imagery.

- Through guided imagery, the healing imagery of dreams can be directed both inward and outward in targeted ways.

As you learn to dialogue with your dreams, you will be cultivating attitudes of openness, trust, receptivity, non-judgment, inclusiveness and, above all, compassion. You will be learning to deepen your relationship to imagery and energies that inspire the heart and stir the soul.

YOUR OWN REFLECTIONS

You can discover deep insights about your own inner world when you truly take on someone else's dream as your own. It is as if you gaze at another's work of art and allow the energies to touch you, or listen to a parable as if it is told just for you.

1. Is there a symbol in Amy's dream that stirs you?

2. What in your life has evoked the anger and fear of a "ticket to some place else"?

3. Where or when in your life have you felt a total loss of control?

4. When have you felt abandoned and all alone?

5. How have you responded in the past to crises situations?

6. How has a crisis changed your life?

7. If you are a caregiver or health professional, express your interest in listening to another's dream. Practice listening to a dream as if it is your own. Instead of offering commentary on the dream, simply reflect back to the dreamer the feelings that are expressed in the dream. "As I am listening and experiencing this dream as my own, I'm feeling angry and afraid." Your compassionate attention is all important.

As you begin to reconnect and work with your own dreams, it is helpful to downshift into a meditative state. You may start by using this script:

Closing your eyes . . . beginning to breathe . . . renewing, relaxing, releasing . . . imagining moving down, down into a centered place within . . . imagining standing before your own wellspring of countless inner resources . . . opening all your senses . . . now extending your cup . . . inviting a dream or "waking" dream experience to come bubbling up . . . reconnecting with the imagery with all of your senses . . . allowing the experience to become a present, living reality . . .

Now, maintaining a state of deep reverie,

1. Write down the dream in the present tense (*I am* sitting, instead of *I was* sitting.)

2. Write down all the feelings in the dream and how you are interacting with the other elements of the dream.

3. Read your dream to yourself. For now, just let the feelings wash over you and savor the dream as a mysterious happening. Hold it lightly as a gift that is waiting to be unwrapped.

2

REMEMBERING AND RECORDING YOUR DREAMS

When crisis strikes, dreams respond with imagery and energy to help the dreamer move through the turmoil. It is as if dreams go into overdrive to focus attention on where the body, mind, or spirit is out of balance and then offer new possibilities for responding.

The night after he was diagnosed with prostate cancer, Sam dreamed about getting ready to go out in his kayak. As a social worker, Sam had worked with many of his own dreams and those of his clients, and he recognized his new dream was similar to others he had called the "Embarking into the Unknown" dreams.

Quandary at the Boat Launch

I'm driving my old pickup down a dusty dirt road.
My prized yellow kayak is in the back. No one is with
me except a little black dog who reminds me of a
mutt I had when I was about ten. I grip the steering
wheel tightly and my whole body bounces as the
truck moves over potholes and uneven gravel. From
the peak of a high incline, I see before me a vast
body of water, a lake larger than I've ever seen before.
Maybe it's an ocean. At this moment the water looks
very still.

I park at the edge of the water by a small dock that looks like a possible place to put in. Tied up are a few canoes and several small outboards, but I don't see even one other kayak or any other people. I'm feeling a little uneasy and now begin to check my backpack. My sense is that I've forgotten something. I feel more confidence when I finger an item that gives me strong assurance. It's my Swiss Army knife.

The dog jumps around barking. I carry the kayak, my backpack, and life jacket down to the edge of the water. Now I'm feeling sure that I've forgotten something. The sun is sinking. Why am I setting out this late in the day and where am I going? I wake up feeling anxious.

Quandary at the Boat Launch is a good dream to demonstrate how one can begin a creative relationship with crisis. The dream brings imagery of Sam's Swiss Army knife, his kayak, his dog and his life jacket. These multi-faceted symbols all hold highly personal meanings for Sam. All are metaphoric images of creative energies he will need for embarking onto the darkening waters of diagnosis, treatment, and their accompanying emotional and spiritual issues.

SAM'S PROCESS

As soon as he woke up, Sam recorded his dream in his journal and made notes about the diagnosis he had received yesterday. He poured a cup of coffee, went to his recliner, closed his eyes, focused on his breathing, and relaxed into a deep meditative state. In imagination, he re-entered his dream. As he re-imagined each symbol, he wrote down his associations.

Kayak: My favorite possession all through college. Took me a year to save for it. Took me on many adventures, some alone, some with friends. Helped me feel responsible for where I was headed. Taught me to stay balanced. Taught me to roll with the rapids. Always brought a sense of exhilaration, often mixed with fear. Taught me to use the currents. Lightweight, easy to carry. Finally cracked up on a bolder in the rapids. I was not seriously injured.

Little black dog: Looks like a mutt I named Star when I was about ten. A bad time for me. Time of my parent's divorce. I could talk to him about my anger and fear when I couldn't seem to bring my parents together. Felt like Star understood me. Unbounded energy. Pooped a lot.

Life jacket: Protection from drowning. Hot. Uncomfortable. Jacket in the dream different from any I ever actually owned. Color is a vivid red.

Swiss Army knife: All-in-one knife with multiple tools. An army knife. Versatile. Sharp. Several blades for cutting. Cork puller, pliers, two screwdrivers, bottle opener, magnifying glass. It is red.

All the dream images Sam listed are symbols that hold energies that may help him relate creatively to his diagnosis and treatment journey.

As a symbol, Kayak can connect Sam with the energy of exhilaration and passion. It can connect him with the energy of persistence, the energy of balance, and the energy for going with the flow. It can reconnect Sam to feelings of responsibility for the direction of his own life. Kayak can remind him to carry his burden lightly, and that in a smash up, he is not seriously injured.

As a symbol, the Black Dog can connect Sam with the power of compassion, understanding, and unconditional love, as well as abundant instinctual energy. The dog can connect Sam with childhood strengths that long ago helped him through his parents' divorce.

The <u>Life Jacket</u> can connect Sam with the energy of protection.

<u>Swiss Army Knife</u> can connect Sam with versatility, flexibility, discernment (ability to cut apart), synthesis (ability to put together), and resources for unexpected needs.

The color <u>Red</u> appears twice, as the color of both the knife and the life jacket. Sam associates passion and life energy with the color red. He also associates red with anger.

SYMBOLS AND PARADOX

Notice that paradox is at the center of every symbol. Symbols hold opposites together, and every symbol contains energies that from an ego perspective feel like opposing energies:

- Sam's kayak holds energies of both exhilaration and fear.

- The dog stirs a sense of loss as well as a sense of connection.

- The life jacket stirs feelings of both protection and discomfort.

- The knife holds energies of both taking apart and putting together.

- Red connects Sam with passion, life energy, and also with anger.

Your personal dream symbols will put you in touch with paradoxical conflict. They will connect you with tensions of multiple opposing perceptions. They also will help you to recognize that light and dark are two sides of the same coin. Danger and opportunity are both a part of crisis. The ability to appreciate the richness of paradox is essential for moving beyond fear and chaos. Transforming fear requires that you open to the gifts of complexity and surprise and nurture attitudes of flexibility and trust. Dreams will bring many experiences in which you can take measure of where you are in relationship to your appreciation of paradox.

Take a moment to meditate with the symbol of the Swiss Army Knife. Close your eyes, breathe, relax, and imagine the knife with all your senses. Where in your life might you need the energies of both cutting apart and putting together?

IMPROVING DREAM RECALL

Sam's dream-work process started with remembering his dream. If you have not had much experience interacting with your dreams, you may feel now that you are, indeed, "embarking into the unknown." Perhaps you are one of many people who remember that they dream but cannot remember *what* they dream. To build relationship with your dreams, you need to be able to remember them. The rest of this chapter will provide practical information and advice about remembering and recording your dreams.

Dream recall usually improves when your goal to remember and to be in relationship with your dreams becomes a top priority. Recall is affected by many factors. Certain medications seem to inhibit memory just as certain others enhance recall. No matter the influences, most people improve dream recall by becoming intentional about remembering. When you are facing critical illness or any crisis, dreams often become very intense and recall may become easier.

Dream recall improves when you prepare. During the day, think often about your hope for a new relationship with your dreams. Get excited and enjoy reading and thinking about dreams. Talk to others about your new interest. Before going to bed, remind yourself that dreams will put you in touch with your deepest self and with imagery and energies that can be used in the healing process. Put passion into your desire to remember and respond.

TIPS TO IMPROVE DREAM RECALL

- Select an evening when you are not overly tired to begin your work with dream recall. When you are exhausted, do not expect to remember dreams, but be grateful for deep sleep.

- Avoid alcohol and caffeine in the evening.

- Avoid strenuous activity right before bed.

- Make bedtime special. Turn off the TV and put reading aside.

- Quietly meditate and review your day for a few minutes:

- What surprised you?

- When did you feel compassionate and connected?

- When did you feel out of sync and disconnected?

- How did today's personal interactions affect your emotions?

- When did you feel gratitude today?

- Try to acknowledge and honor all your feelings. Your dreams will respond to your bedtime reflections.

GET READY TO RECEIVE

- Have a journal or small recorder next to your bed. A tiny light or a lighted pen can be helpful.

- Write down the date in your dream journal. You may want to create a special journal as a symbol of your commitment to the dream relationship, but any notebook will serve. You may prefer to record on a voice recorder.

- Record any emotionally important situation in your life at the time.

- Focus on your intention. Express appreciation for the dialogue. Develop your own positive bedtime rituals about remembering your dreams. You may, for example, affirm that you will wake up after each dream and record key images. Make your affirmations succinct and positive. "I will remember and record my dreams tonight."

- After affirming your intent to remember a dream, you may also want to write a request for a dream experience that will help bring clarity to an issue. You can also make a request for support and guidance. Chapters 7 and 9 elaborate on the process of initiating a dream.

- If you have ignored your dreams for many years, there may be resistance to remembering. Think of the development of dream dialogue as the development of dialogue with someone who speaks a foreign language. It will require discipline and practice. The more you practice, the easier the communication. Trust the power of intention and imagination. Be excited about beginning to dialogue with a realm of inner support and wisdom.

- As you go to sleep, you might imagine yourself dreaming. You might imagine being in the company of the "Dream Maker" or in the company of a helpful dream character. Perhaps imagine writing down your dream the next morning. Try different imaginal scenarios and see what feels helpful. Imagine being in relationship with the realm of the dream. Have fun with this!

ESTABLISH GOOD DREAM HABITS

- Make a commitment to record your dreams whenever you wake during the night instead of waiting until morning.

- Make a commitment to write down dream fragments. Every "snippet" is important.

- Write down the feelings or emotions you experienced *in* the dream. These may be very different from your emotions upon awakening. Attitudes and feelings *in* the dream can be a strong clue as to what is needed for healing and expanded living.

- Record the action and interactions. How are you and others responding and relating?

- Dreams are very ephemeral and most tend to disappear almost immediately. If you go back to sleep without recording a dream, you probably will not remember it in the morning. This is a common occurrence, even among experienced dream workers.

- If you have to set an alarm clock, set it on soft music. Nothing makes a dream vanish quicker than a loud, shrill alarm clock.

ON AWAKENING

- Lie still. Avoid running to the bathroom or even turning over. Relax and let your mind dwell on dreams or dream fragments. Let the energies of the dream affect you. Begin to tell the dream to yourself in your mind, translating the images and feelings into words.

- Pay particular attention to your feelings and impressions, and to the sensations in your body.

- Start with whatever part of the dream you remember and let the details come back to you. Sometimes it is easier to start with the end of a dream and work your way backwards. Alternatively, start with your feelings and work your way into the dream.

- Now you can try gently changing positions. This often triggers memories of dreams you had while in that position. Give yourself a few minutes of quiet reflection to let the dream elements come to you in each position.

- Review the dream in your mind before attempting to record it. If this is during the middle of the night, at least write down or record a few key words or phrases that are likely to trigger your memory in the morning.

RECORDING YOUR DREAMS

In the morning or as soon as you can, expand any notes you have made in the night. Reconnect with the dream by closing your eyes and breathing deeply into a relaxed state. As you relax, move back into the dream. Explore the details with all of your senses. Open to the emotions in the dream. Before you record, feel into the mystery of the experience.

- Date your journal entry or speak the date if you are recording. Leave space for a title. **(For the purposes of this book, dream dates have been omitted; but for tracking purposes, it is very important to put a date on each dream.)**

- Write down the dream as quickly as you can without judging or editing. Record everything you remember, even things that seem inconsequential or nonsensical.

- Record in the present tense. (*I am running, instead of I was running.*) Writing in the present tense will take you back to the immediacy of the dream every time you read it.

- Sketch some of the images if you like.

- Go back and give your dream a title or headline. Use key symbols that will later help trigger memory of the entire dream. For example, instead of "Someone Chases Me," be specific: "Bearded Man in Purple Jacket Chases Me Down NY City Alley."

- Be sure to record impressions, attitudes, and feelings, as well as descriptions. Remember to stick with the attitudes and feelings **in** the dream. Do not censor or reject any impressions or emotional responses.

- Record colors right away. They tend to "evaporate" quickly.

- Record the action carefully. How are you relating to the other elements of the dream and how are they relating to each other? Record the action and the ways you are interacting. Perhaps you are just observing.

- Make sure you write down the main symbols: characters, setting, outstanding objects, colors, etc. You may want to underline these key symbols as you go.

- As you record the dream, notice but do not change misspellings, odd word choices, or unintended puns. When you write quickly without censoring, the unconscious freely supplies additional data that will help when you are exploring the dream. Make sure to record what is happening in waking life at the time of the dream.

- Again, if you do not recall a dream, record your first thoughts or body sensations upon awakening. Talk to the Dream Maker or whatever you want to call the source of the dream. This is a dialogue. Express your disappointment in not remembering a dream and your hope for remembering, your hope and intention for continuing the dialogue and building a relationship with the source of the dream and the mysterious realm of possibility beyond the conscious ego.

- Make a response in your dream journal every morning. Many dreamers are now using the computer to record and reflect upon their dreams. Whatever medium you choose, nurture each day your growing sense of relationship with energy of deep support and wisdom. Whether you remember a dream or not, journal from your heart about your deepest needs and hopes.

MAKING AN INDEX

Designate several pages in the back of your journal as an Index. Record the date and title of each dream in the Index. Include the primary symbols and also the actions in your entry. Record your responses including emotions and attitudes. The Index will help bring the dream back to memory even years from now. You can use the Index to review recurring symbols, emotions, and responses, and to notice themes as they develop. The Index will help you track growth in your relationship to the realm of deep wisdom as it unfolds, transforms, and expands. If you are recording on the computer, you can use your computer's search capabilities. You can even use one of the many software programs that have been developed for recording and tracking your dreams.

SAM'S INDEX ENTRY

<u>Quandary at the Boat Launch</u>: Driving old pickup, black dog, yellow kayak, feeling unease, finding Swiss Army knife, feeling more confident, feeling alone and insecure, no panic, sun sinking. Another embarking into the unknown.

Sam reported to the dream circle that according to his Index, his *Quandary at the Boat Launch* was his fourth dream in the past year with the theme "Embarking into the Unknown." He also said he was somewhat encouraged by this dream because in spite of feeling a bit anxious, there were no signs of the extreme panic reaction he had experienced in his other *embarking* dreams. Also there were good feelings about the presence of the dog and the Swiss Army knife.

YOUR OWN PRE-DREAM APPRECIATION SURVEY

Engaging with dreams is a way of being in touch with a source of deep wisdom and support. Please take some time to reflect on where you are on your own journey. Remember that dreams are responses to your deepest conflicts and also to your heart's deepest longings. Begin with these questions:

- Are you facing a current crisis?

- Where do you feel blocked and stuck?

- What worries you, causes anxiety?

- What are the contents of your fears?

- Which of your personal relationships are shaky?

- Where do you feel unsupported?

- Where in your life do you feel the most conflicted?

- What is your purpose in life? What are your goals in reaching your purpose?

- What are the barriers that block you? How might you move through the barriers?

- What are your passions? What makes your heart sing?

- What images, emotions, interactions, or themes keep recurring in your dreams?

Make a list of your strengths. Circle the ones that have become hard to access. List additional strengths that you would like to develop.

Make a commitment to record and to develop a deep relationship with the images and sensations that come to you through your dreams.

Make a commitment to learn how to downshift into a meditative state of consciousness.

Make a commitment to bring the wisdom and healing energies of your dreams into your present life.

Complete this sentence: I hope that my dreams will . . . .

PADDLING ON

Over the next few days, Sam continued to engage with his kayak dream. Before going to bed, he breathed and relaxed into a meditative space. In his re-entry meditations, he launched the kayak and began to paddle into the sunset. In each meditation he felt the bodily sensations of becoming more balanced and centered as he plunged the paddle into the water from one side to the other. He felt the warm companionship of the dog and the security of the versatile knife in his pocket.

Sam allowed the dream to evolve and develop. He told the group that as the sun went down, a full moon appeared over the water. In one unusually vivid dream re-entry experience, a highly focused stream of moonlight enveloped him.

Sam credits his dream meditations with helping him maintain a fairly consistent positive outlook during his radiation treatments. As he lay under the radiation machine, Sam re-imagined the beam of light from the full moon coming into his body. He imagined the beam penetrating his prostate gland, shrinking the cancer. Sam reported that with each imagery journey, he felt more connected and at peace.

MOVING INTO A MEDITATIVE STATE

Whenever you engage with a dream, as Sam has demonstrated, you will first want to drop into a meditative state of consciousness, an in-between state where the logical, verbal brain can easily connect with the intuitive, sensate brain. Before writing the dream down, before journaling about your feelings and associations, you will want to downshift. Once you are back in your dream, you may also want to imagine the dream moving backward or forward in time so that your experience is expanded. You may want to clarify colors, time of day, or other vague details of the dream.

Most important, you may want to re-enter a dream to participate in transformation of a nightmare. As you allow the dream to develop, it can become a new dream. Then, in a meditative state with guided imagery, you can direct the transformed energy into your body, mind, and spirit. You can also direct the transformed energy outward to others or toward the healing of an outer-life situation.

The first step is to focus on the natural rhythm of your breath. As you relax with each breath, you will move into a state in which the body responds with a decrease in heart rate, breathing rate, blood pressure, and metabolic rate—the exact opposite of the fight or flight response. For several decades, research has shown that relaxation is at the core of most meditative practices.[1]

The following script will help you to progressively relax each part of your body so that you can move into a centered place within. You may download this script with background music from our website, www.healingpowerofdreams. Background music usually enhances the impact of the experience. If you record the script for yourself or have someone else read it to you, allow short pauses between the dots and long pauses between the paragraphs. With practice, you may find you can shortcut many of the steps, and can drop down into a deeply relaxed, focused state almost instantly. Allow yourself to relax even as you read the script. Each time you practice, you will find it easier to downshift. A copy of this script can be found in the Appendix.

A word of caution: If at any time you begin to feel disturbed during the relaxation exercise, simply open your eyes and discontinue. You are in control at all times and can choose to participate in the exercise or not.

SCRIPT 1: GUIDED IMAGERY FOR DEEP RELAXATION

Begin by closing your eyes if that's comfortable . . . whether sitting or lying down, aligning your body so energy can flow freely . . . breathing naturally while moving your attention inside . . . connecting with the breath . . . renewing with each inhale . . . releasing with each exhale . . . breathing in . . . breathing out . . . drawing in the warm energy of renewal . . . and with each out-breath, releasing whatever needs to be released . . . breath moving in . . . breath moving out . . . with each breath relaxing deeper and deeper into a centered place within . . . all the inner fragments becoming still and quiet . . .

Now checking in with your body . . . sending the warm energy of the breath to any place that needs special care . . . moving your focus to your toes . . . allowing your toes to relax . . . all ten toes . . .

and moving your attention through your feet . . . allowing both feet to soften and relax . . . and moving attention through your ankles . . . and through your lower legs . . . your knees . . . your thighs . . . and into your buttocks and hips . . . sinking more deeply into the support of whatever you're sitting or lying on . . . and now checking in with your trunk . . . breathing into the pelvic region . . . bringing in the breath of renewal . . . releasing whatever is needing to be released . . . and into your abdomen . . . up through your solar plexus . . . into your chest . . . your heart . . . your lungs . . . with each breath, filling with renewal all the way up to your collar bones . . . and releasing whatever needs to be released . . .

Now moving your attention around the sides of your body and into your back . . . breathing into your lower back from your tail bone . . . through the sacrum . . . your lower back . . . mid back . . . into your upper back . . . noticing your shoulder blades and the space between your shoulder blades . . . and now your shoulders and down through your arms and hands . . . noticing both hands . . . your fingers and thumbs . . . your palms and the backs of your hands . . . and through your wrists . . . lower arms . . . elbows . . . upper arms and back into your shoulders . . . and now checking in with your neck . . . breathing in warmth and renewal . . allowing any place that needs tending to loosen and soften . . . all through your neck and throat relaxing, releasing . . . and now noticing your head . . . allowing the back of your scalp to relax . . . all across the top of your scalp . . . your forehead . . . all around your eyes . . . your cheeks . . . all around your mouth . . . your chin . . . your eyes heavy in their sockets . . . your tongue soft and heavy in your mouth . . . noticing your entire body.

Breathing in, renewing . . . breathing out, releasing, relaxing . . . moving into a deeply centered place within . . . resting in a place of deep harmony and balance at the center of your being . . . ready now to connect with your dream.[2]

YOUR OWN REFLECTIONS

Before you read farther, begin to engage with a symbol in your dreams that strikes your attention and evokes strong emotion. Close your eyes, connect with your breathing, allow yourself to sink into deep relaxation. Invite an image from a dream to appear. Whatever image bubbles up, even if you do not remember it as a dream image, welcome it into your meditative space. Now savor the image with all of your senses. Feel the energies of the symbol in your body.

Quickly write down your associations including your feelings and any thoughts or memories the symbol evokes. Use Sam's dream reflections as a model.

After writing your associations, ask yourself:

1. Where might I need the energies of this symbol in my present life?

2. Do any of my associations to this symbol present themselves as opposites?

3. Do these opposing energies show up any place in my waking life?

4. Can I imagine balancing these opposites?

5. If you are a caregiver or health professional, after listening to the dream of another with total non-judgmental attention, you may want to remark, "If this were my dream, I'd wonder how this dream is trying to help me live my life in an expanded way?"

3
DREAM APPRECIATION PRACTICES

In the Healing Power of Dreams project, we encourage participants to relate to the dream as a work of art, rather than as a puzzle to be solved. The goal is to ponder the dream and to stir the imagery until the energies that lead to healing and growth begin to emerge.

EMILY

Emily's dreams with their particular symbols have become the medium through which she is able to work on a crisis that has developed with Andrew, her partner for the past five years. One year ago Emily completed treatment for cervical cancer. Though she soon went back to work, she has continued to come to the cancer center to attend the weekly dream circle, yoga classes, and writing workshops. At the beginning of her treatment, Emily developed a practice of daily journaling. Every morning she writes down her dreams and sits with the images in a short meditation. Before bed, she relaxes into a meditative state and journals about how her dreams weave with her waking world. For two nights last December, Emily wrote about her depression.

> Holiday time stirs up depression every year. Why this unrelenting load of heaviness? I'm back on my feet. Totally recovered from the cancer experience,

so they say. But I feel weighted down. Each step an act of will. Can't believe it's been a year since my surgery and the awful clinical trial that seemed to go on forever. Can't believe I'm back at work and getting promotions and being treated like completely well and competent person. No one seems to suspect the ravages of my anxiety, the surprise terror attacks that nearly buckle my knees, the pieces of myself that careen off in twenty different directions. No one suspects the smoldering anger of my unloved body parts that were cast off like resented children and scream to be remembered.

No one knows about Andrew's restlessness. Dear Andrew. Please don't leave me now! Or is it time? Have we come to the end of being together? You were so faithful all through my cancer, so loving. I couldn't have survived without you. We've been partners now for five years, totally committed to each other, happy most of the time. Weren't we? You said the cancer brought us even closer together. I know it's been hard. Is it that you really want children even though you've said all along that it doesn't make any difference? Last night when I brought up the topic of getting married and adopting a child, you walked away without speaking. Please, Andrew. I don't want us to end.

The next morning, Emily recorded the following dream:

Tarnished and Abandoned

I'm in our kitchen sorting through a drawer of flat silverware pieces that were handed down to me from my grandmother. All the pieces are turning black with tarnish. A flood of memories wells up and I feel a great longing to restore their sheen. As I rub the silver pieces with a soft cloth, I become calm. Then Andrew crosses the room and without looking at

me or speaking, just walks out the back door. I feel
a sense of panic and tremendous grief. I wake up
crying.

In the Index section at the back of her dream journal, Emily
wrote,

> Tarnished and Abandoned: longing to restore sheen,
> rubbing with soft cloth, feeling connection with
> Grandmother, Andrew walks out. Panic! Grief!

After writing the dream, Emily sat quietly with the images. She
allowed herself to feel her emotion. She re-imagined the pain and
panic. She re-imagined polishing with the soft cloth.

SYMBOLS AND METAPHORS

With your own dreams, focus first on how you are feeling in the
dream. Focus on your emotions. Notice your attitudes and how you
are interacting and responding in the dream. Keep these key questions
in mind:

1. What in my life feels like this?

2. Where in my life do I or did I respond in this way?

3. Is this a limiting or life expanding experience?

Sit quietly with the dream. Feel the atmosphere and the emotions
of the total impact. Let the energies stir you. Where in your body are

you feeling the emotions? Keep reconnecting with your breath and intentionally relaxing, allowing the images to move and shift as living entities. Stay open to the mystery.

At some point, after pondering the overall effect, you will also want to explore some of the discrete symbols of your dream. "A symbol is something that represents something else by association, resemblance or convention, especially a material object used to represent something invisible" (American Heritage Dictionary). A good example is the American flag with all its multiple meanings to various people. For most WW II veterans, the flag evoked pride; for some Vietnam War protesters, it stirred anger and disrespect. Like the flag, the images in dreams are symbols that carry many simultaneous multiple meanings on multiple levels. In dreams, the images are symbols of complex combinations of emotions, perceptions and thoughts. Your approach will be to write down all your many feelings, memories, and associations that your symbols stir up for you.

In his book, *Dream Language*, dream expert Robert J. Hoss helps us to understand the symbolic and metaphoric nature of dream imagery as he summarizes and synthesizes recent research on the dreaming brain. Modern imaging techniques reveal that during REM sleep, when most dreaming occurs, rational and logical thinking, sequential organization, planning, and working memory parts of the brain are inactive. For the most part, outside input and executive functions are shut down. The visual association area is active, and imagery is selected and created according to emotional associations, memories, inner meanings, and contextual references. Most active during REM are areas that process emotion, engage in analogical conflict resolutions and problem solving, and produce picture metaphors, which represent the material being processed within. These patterns of brain activation help us understand that almost all dream imagery originates from within, images in dreams are indeed symbols, and the language of dreams is the language of metaphor. Dream imagery mirrors inner emotional associations that are contextually related to outer life situations.[1]

Hoss says that metaphors in dreams are "analogies drawn between the dream story and your waking life story." The language of dreams is "a language of visual imagery and association in which combinations of images identify our thoughts and experiences, rather than combinations of letters and words." When we tell or write a dream, "images are translated (by our verbal language centers) into word associations or figures of speech," that is, metaphors. For example, if you dream that you are playing in a ball game but cannot hold onto the ball, you may not understand what the dream is saying until you tell the dream or record it in your journal—"then suddenly I dropped the ball." This is the metaphor, the analogy between your dream story and your waking life story. Now you can understand that the dream is not commenting on your ball-playing skill but is asking you to look for a place in your waking life where you feel you are "dropping the ball," that is failing to do what you need to do.[2]

Symbols are like the visible, outer clothing for invisible energetic networks of emotions, memories, perceptions, intellectual constructs, desires, and combinations of all the above. They are metaphoric expressions of personally relevant associations. Dream symbols usually appear as recognizable objects, though they are often bizarre to be sure. The bizarre nature of a symbol such as a flying cat or talking lamp reflects the psyche's ability to synthesize simultaneous multiple associations.

Every symbol is like a bridge to multiple meanings. Symbols join the literal and the metaphoric. Symbols connect the conscious and unconscious realms. Symbols form bridges from the familiar to the unknown, from the material realm to the invisible. They also carry relational energy and connect you with a sense of depth, meaning and mystery. As we saw with Sam's dream, symbols serve as natural attempts to reconcile conflicted feelings of opposing dynamics.

SYMBOL APPRECIATION

Emily used the following guidelines to begin to explore her most evocative dream symbol, the flat silverware. She recorded these directions, questions, and responses in her journal:

Describe your symbol as if to clarify it for someone who is not familiar with the image.

> I have a big drawer of flat silver we never use that
> I inherited from my grandmother. There are about
> 100 knives, forks, spoons, and serving utensils in all,
> and now the pieces are all jumbled together and are
> tarnished and black from neglect.

Now reflect on your symbol with the following ten questions. You may write your responses or speak them out loud.

1. **What is its function?**

> This silver is supposed to have more than a
> utilitarian use. Its function was to add graciousness
> to every meal. My grandmother used her flat
> silverware every day along with good linens and
> china. She kept the silver polished and shining so
> that every meal was like a feast for royalty.

2. **What do you feel about it?**

> I feel guilty that I have neglected to use and take care
> of this treasure. I feel a strong urge to bring back the
> sheen.

3. **What do you associate with it?**

My grandmother, elegant meals, treasure, being special, valuable, durable, being part of a family, belonging, childhood. My strongest association is my feeling of tarnished femininity since the hysterectomy. Also, I now fear that the relationship with Andrew is tarnished.

4. **What does it remind you of?**

I was a princess at my grandmother's table. I was happy being special. I loved the family gatherings. I realize I never go out of my way to bring beauty and grace to my table with Andrew.

5. **What do you like and dislike about it?**

I love that I inherited this treasure. I hate that I have neglected to use it and have let it become tarnished.

6. **What body sensations do you feel when reflecting on the symbol?**

I feel sadness in my heart and anticipation all through my gut; a loss of energy when I see the tarnish, then a surge of energy when I start to polish it.

7. **To what is the symbol a bridge in waking life? What in your life resonates with the feelings and associations and responses?**

The tarnished silver in my dream is a bridge to the forgotten inheritance of strong support I felt from my grandmother. It's a bridge to my feelings about my tarnished feminine essence. The silverware is also a bridge to my present feelings of guilty neglect and abandonment. I know I feel these conflicts in the relationship with Andrew.

8. **What are the insights and energies this symbol brings?**

The silverware heightens awareness of my doubts about my self-worth and yet connects me with remembering how much love I've received. It stirs a sense of and reinforces my hope for resolution with Andrew. I can feel the tension between fear and belonging.

9. **Go back and "feel into" the entire dream. Keep asking:**

What does this dream want?

How can these images and energies contribute to the enlargement of my relationship to myself, to others, and to the dream's creative energy?

What old patterns do I need to release so that I can heal and grow?

What is the new direction the dream is pointing to?

This dream wants me to deal with my fear that Andrew might leave. The tarnished silver triggers my sense of guilty neglect, my insecurity and self-doubt; but also brings solid feelings of being loved. I think the dream wants me to make use of both my actual and symbolic resources for taking in nourishment and for setting a graceful table for myself and others. I think the dream wants me to own my grief about the limitations of my body and my doubts about my feminine self-worth since the hysterectomy. I think it wants me to polish my tarnished connection with family and all the love I've inherited. I think it wants me to move past my fear and claim the luster of my feminine essence. It wants me to trust that the relationship with Andrew can once more shine. And if it doesn't—to know I can find my way through the loss, like I found my way through the cancer. I can find a new way to be untarnished with myself.

10. **How can you honor this dream? How can you bring the new energies and insights of the dream into your waking life?**

First I'll go back to the part of the dream when I am polishing the silver with the soft cloth. I'll meditate with the sensate experience of polishing, and I'll feel myself carefully restoring each piece. As the dark tarnish disappears, I'll take in the expanding luster as blessing for myself and for everyone I love. And I'll try to stay connected to this growing shine. When I talk to Andrew I'll listen. I rarely listen deeply with my full attention. I don't even listen to myself. I rarely ask Andrew about his work anymore. Dear Andrew, I'll try to be fully present— both to myself and to you. Please, please, I'll try.

A few days later, Emily recorded the following in her journal:

Andrew's office is laying off people left and right. No certainty he won't be next. For months I've chattered mindlessly about my successes at my office with no thought he might be in a precarious position. Now I realize how much my insensitivity has been hurting him. Cautiously we're talking about us—sharing the grief about our infertility and slowly circling around the question of marriage. If only we can keep dreaming . . .

Reflect on Emily's dream as if it is your own.

- In your own life, for what might the tarnished silverware be a good metaphor?

- What might be a way that you can polish and restore the tarnished silver in your own life?

- How can you be more fully present, both to yourself and to others?

MORE SUGGESTIONS FOR ENGAGING YOUR DREAMS

As you begin to engage with your dreams, pay attention to dreams about people or situations from the past. It is likely that by reminding you of the past, the dream is trying to help you respond to a present or future situation in a more life-expanding way. How is the reminder of the past a possible clue to a better direction in your present or future?

Pay attention to words that are spoken or seen in the dream. Words may have a literal message, but they will also have broader metaphorical meanings as well, probably on multiple levels.

Pay attention to bizarre and quirky elements. List all your associations. Look for the metaphors, and ask the key questions: What in my life feels like this? Where in my life do I respond in this way? Bizarre symbols often help reveal conflict and usually offer important clues for moving toward paradoxical synthesis.

Pay attention to colors. Almost always, colors can bring insight into your emotional dynamics. They contribute to the emotional atmosphere. Reflect on what feelings the colors stir up and what in your life you associate with the colors.[3]

Pay attention to babies and children. Sometimes un-integrated "shadow" energies show up in dreams as children. They invite you to explore undeveloped creative energies. Babies often help connect you with emerging new dynamics, with potential that is ready to be acknowledged and expressed. Children often lead to insights and energies about your own childhood. Feel into the energies of each dream child and discern the unique energies each carries. Let dream children be your guides to expanded possibilities.

Pay attention to animals: Animals can teach you to recognize your instinctual, intuitive capacities and guide you into expanded relationship with the "animal" parts of yourself and others. Feel into the nature of each particular dream creature. Ponder the gifts of each one's unique energies. Animals often serve as guides and mediators of encounters with healing presence.

Pay attention to settings. Settings offer metaphorical reflections of emotional, mental, spiritual, and physical states of being. All settings carry emotional atmosphere. Ask what in your life stirs up the same feelings that the setting stirs up. Often the setting helps pinpoint a time and place where a specific network of feelings began. At the same time, settings can spur memories of past experiences and bring energies that can help you with present and future issues. Look for metaphors that resonate with your present condition as you write out your associations.

Pay attention to houses and other dwellings. Your associations to dream houses and dwellings often mirror the state of your body, psyche, or lifestyle. Notice details of each particular house and reflect on them as metaphors. Notice if any part of the house is in need of repair or is an unusually welcoming dwelling space.

Pay attention to cars and other vehicles. As symbols, they may help you recognize how you are presently moving through your life, and may help you get in touch with a part of yourself that is in need of physical or emotional attention. Is every part of the car functioning properly? Notice your relationship with the car or vehicle. Are you driving? Are you the owner? What are the energies of each particular dream car or vehicle? How do the energies you associate with the car manifest in your waking life?

Pay attention to recurring dreams. A recurring dream usually indicates there is an unresolved issue that you are repeatedly ignoring. Recurrence is a way of highlighting the importance of what is in need of attention. Sometimes, recurrence points to unacknowledged strengths and resources. Recurrence is an invitation to move into a more life-giving way of responding.

Pay attention to dreams that bring a sense of healing. These are dreams that leave you with a sense of renewal and reconciliation, a sense of awe and wonder. These are dreams that leave you feeling acceptance and peace. Healing dreams bring potent symbols that can become the focus for guided imagery. The imagery can be directed toward healing of the body, mind, and spirit. Healing dreams provide immediate "dream medicine" and will be the focus of Chapter 7.

Pay attention to nightmares. Nightmares are a straight path to an aspect of your life that needs your immediate attention. You will learn there are many ways to transform their energies.

DISCOVERING THEMES

You don't have to dialogue with your dreams very long before you realize that your dream stories can be grouped into recurring themes. The scenarios may differ, but the theme, the basic pattern of the dream, shows up over and over again.

> Looking back at the Index entries for their dreams, members of the dream circle discovered these themes:
>
> Ticket to Someplace Else: Wanting to go home, tropical airport, menacing Ticket Seller, sold ticket to unwanted destination, colorful native people, children playing, sense of being totally alone, terrified. **Theme**: Terror and sense of aloneness in midst of colorful, resourceful others.
>
> Quandary at the Boat Launch: Driving old pickup, black dog, yellow kayak, unease, finding Swiss Army knife, feel alone and insecure, sun sinking, where am I going? **Theme:** Embarking into unknown—again. Less panic this time.
>
> Tarnished and Abandoned: Sorting, longing to restore sheen, rubbing with soft cloth, feeling connection with Grandmother, Andrew walks out. Panic! Grief! **Theme:** Conflict between fear of losing and acceptance of support and loving inheritance.

In reviewing her Index, Emily saw the theme "fear of losing" in three recent dreams. The dream about the tarnished silverware presented another theme, "inherited family strengths." After identifying this theme, Emily began to notice symbols of unacknowledged family resources both within and all around her. These symbols became focal points for her guided imagery meditations. She meditated with the image of her father's pipe to connect with his and her own strong sense of humor. She meditated with the image of a piece of her mother's knitting to connect with her own talent to knit together seemingly unrelated ideas into a meaningful synthesis. She meditated with the image of her aunt's garden hoe and felt her own love for planting seeds, especially seeds of ideas for new magazine articles. Meditating with her grandfather's pen stirred her passion for writing. All these symbols brought healing energy into Emily's daily practice.

Amy began recording her dreams shortly after joining the dream circle. After she had recorded ten dreams, she reviewed them and wrote down tentative ideas for themes: Feeling alone and unsupported; unaware of possible resources; bright colors; hoping to be rescued.

TRACKING FEELINGS AND INTERACTIONS

In cancer groups, participants look for themes that indicate change and growth toward healing and wholeness. The focus is on response patterns and interactions. This means paying close attention to all the feelings, attitudes, perceptions—and particularly paying attention to the behaviors, the actions, the adverbs and verbs.

The focus on feelings and interactions provides a personal barometer for tracking changes in your relationships to the multiple layers of your life. For example, in Amy's ticket dream, her fear reaction was an accurate measure of her relationship to her diagnosis and to her family and work relationships. In later dreams, Amy was less fearful, and she could see the change as a reflection of her changing responses to her illness and relationship challenges.

Focusing on feelings and interactions also helps you to see new possibilities for expanding and deepening your sense of healing. For example, Amy caught a glimpse of her own capacity for playfulness and lightheartedness through the children and native travelers in her dream. Sam's memories of his own abiding resources were triggered by symbols of the kayak, dog, backpack, and Swiss Army knife. The progression of positive attitudes through dreams and guided imagery exercises reflects energy that has become available for recovery and growth, as is shown in current neuroscience research. Numerous studies affirm the brain's remarkable power to change its own structure. REM sleep, when most dreaming occurs, provides ideal conditions for neuroplastic change. Furthermore, positive changes in dream imagery and positive movement in dream themes have been shown to reflect not only the brain's incredible ability to re-wire itself but also the dreamer's emotional growth.[4]

If you are able to participate in a dream circle or somehow to share your dreams with others, you will quickly begin to realize the commonalty of dream themes, no matter the dreamer's background or culture.[5] Your sense of connection with others will strengthen and grow as you realize that the broad themes of the healing journey are similar for everyone and that dream imagery moves in a direction of wholeness for anyone who begins to tend imagery that comes from within.

Begin to track your feelings and interactions in your dreams. This will give you an opportunity to see how you are moving away from fear into confidence and strength. You can track movement from fragmentation toward synthesis, from despair to hope, from rejection to compassion. You can track your sense of an ever-deepening, ever-expanding sense of relationship with yourself, with others, and with your spiritual life.

TIPS FOR IDENTIFYING THE THEME

Distilling a theme is an art, and some dreams have more than one theme. There is no right or wrong way to track the patterns of how you respond to your life. The hope is that you will become increasingly aware that your dreams spotlight unconscious patterns in symbolic and metaphoric ways. Once patterns become conscious, you can transform and integrate them for your healing and growth.

- Be patient. In the beginning, simply record the date and the title of the dream in your Index.

- List the main symbols (images). These will be mostly nouns and adjectives—tarnished silver, old pickup. Then list the feelings, attitudes—how you are responding in the dream and how the other elements of the dream are interacting. These will be the verbs and adverbs.

- Review your Index frequently. Recurring patterns help identify themes. If you record your dreams on a computer, you can use automatic search capabilities to help you.

- Pay particular attention to recurring attitudes and feelings. For example, Emily counted six "fear of loss" dreams in one month.

- Pay attention to recurring actions and interactions. Example: Amy counted three dreams in which she was threatened by another character in the dream and tried to get away.

- When you as the dreamer feel fear or any other strong feeling in the dream, make note of how another character in the dream may be responding in a different or even opposite way. Example: Amy was terrified in her ticket dream. The children were playing and the natives displayed a holiday mood. We will later explore the concept that all the characters in a dream, at least on one level, reflect potential aspects of you, the dreamer, and that you may find energies that you need through other characters in your dream.

- Notice shifts in feelings, attitudes, and responses in each dream and from dream to dream. Examples: Sam noticed a dramatically decreased level of panic in his most recent dream. Emily commented to the dream circle that this was her first "fear of losing" dream that was paired with feelings of appreciation.

YOUR OWN REFLECTIONS

Choose a dream symbol that holds a lot of energy for you. Describe it and play with the symbol appreciation questions below. Reflect on the collage that emerges. When writing your responses, use abbreviations. No one else will see your journal. Keep the symbol alive through meditation. Note that your responses may keep changing. Remember that imagery is like outer clothing for energy and is always changing.

1. Re-imagine your symbol. Describe it as if for someone who has no concept of what it is. Then reflect: What is its function, especially in the dream? What are your associations? What memories does it stir? What do you like and dislike about the symbol? What do you feel in your body as you imagine the symbol?

2. How are you responding or interacting with the symbol in the dream? Is this a different response from what you would make in waking life? Is anyone else in the dream responding in a different way?

3. How is this symbol a bridge to waking life? Where or when in your life did you or do you feel the same as you feel with this symbol? Do any of your written associations to the symbol resonate as metaphors?

4. What insights does the symbol bring? Does it help you to identify a perception, belief, attitude, or pattern of behavior you might need to let go in order to move into an expanded way of being?

5. Do your insights connect you with one of your themes? For example, Amy became aware that the happy children in her dream might be possibilities within herself. This insight connected her with a recurring pattern of "not noticing or nurturing her inner child." Does your symbol connect you with a recurring pattern in your life?

6. How can you honor this symbol by bringing its insights and energies into your waking life?

7. Hold your symbol in meditation. Open all your senses. Savor the energies. Allow the imagery to shift and move. Allow the insights and energies to impact your body, mind, and soul.

8. Let gratitude touch you. Express appreciation as you move deeper into relationship with the energies of the dream. Take time to meditate with the mystery that is stirring and opening your heart.

9. Several times a week, make a list of imagery that stirs a sense of gratitude. Just before bedtime when you are reviewing your day is a good time to do this since you will then carry the energy of gratitude into your dreams.

10. If you are a caregiver or health professional, after listening attentively to a dream, you can help the dreamer gain insight by simply asking for the dreamer to tell you more about key symbols. Encourage the dreamer to make associations. Your role is to be a supportive witness. You do not need to interpret or "fix."

4
NIGHTMARE TRANSFORMATION

Literally and metaphorically, nightmares wake us up. We remember them because we are frightened. Nightmares are dreams that give us a "heads up" that something is out of balance and in need of repair. It may be something we have been ignoring, neglecting, repressing, or denying, and a nightmare may be our first understanding that something is wrong.

A few weeks before she was diagnosed with ovarian cancer, Margaret woke from an upsetting nightmare.

Rotting Bird and Giant Snake

I feel a sense of foreboding as I stand at the top of my basement stairs. An ominous smell wafts up from the darkness. I hate going down to investigate the source, but know that I'm the only one here to do it. I feel increasingly anxious as I descend and the odor grows stronger. The smell seems to be coming from the area where I've stacked several storage boxes. On top of the boxes is an old purse. It's hanging open, and as I get closer, I can tell this must be the source. I don't want to touch the purse, so I climb up on a stool to see inside. A dead bird has almost completely rotted inside. I feel a stab of horror, jump from the stool,

and hurry back up the stairs. A giant black snake is
blocking the doorway at the top. I wake up terrified
and soaked with sweat.

Margaret found she could not ignore this frightening dream. It
kept going round and round in her head, churning up fear each time
it surfaced. She shared the dream with several people. Still it plagued
her. One friend said she had read an article about dreams predicting
illnesses and suggested she go to a doctor for a check-up. Margaret was
lucky. She went to her internist. After a complete examination, he
sent her to an oncologist who found an early stage cancer. Margaret
was able to start treatment immediately. Over time, she has learned
that many other women have dreamed specifically of "rot" before their
diagnosis of cancer. There are many accounts of dreams that alert the
dreamer to something that is not only emotionally or spiritually out
of balance, but also to something that is physiologically wrong.[1]

Jay, who is recovering from thyroid cancer, shares two nightmares
that were loud pleas to stop smoking.

Kids Trapped in Smoky Room

My two kids are trapped in their smoke-filled
playroom. They are banging on the door and
screaming hysterically. Smoke is seeping under the
door. I wake up trying to break the door down.

Black X-Ray

I'm in my doctor's office, and he hands me an
x-ray. On it, my lungs are totally black. I wake up
frightened and knowing for sure that this dream is
saying something critical.

After these nightmares, Jay stopped smoking. A few months later, before his diagnosis of thyroid cancer, Jay had several more nightmares about attacks on his throat. In the first dream, hundreds of bees were stinging his neck in the throat area. In another, a "threatening enemy" was sticking needles into his throat. In other dreams he was trying to speak, but no sound would come out. Jay looks back on these nightmares as clear attempts to alert him to his cancer.[2]

Like Jay and Margaret, other survivors report pre-diagnosis nightmares as well as intense dreams throughout the treatment journey, including frightening nightmares about dying. It is understandable to want to get rid of a nightmare. Nightmares disrupt quality sleep which is essential to the healing process. Nightmare energy even lingers into daylight hours, damping down moods and feelings.

Even so, nightmares can be powerful allies in the healing journey. Like Margaret's dream with the rotting bird, a nightmare can alert the dreamer to a pending crisis, offering a chance to act and influence the outcome. A disturbing dream can also provide the images and energies that with dream appreciation and guided imagery techniques can be used to transform the nightmare into a healing dream.

GROUNDED IN RESEARCH

The nightmare research of Earnest Hartmann, M.D. demonstrates that the central image of any nightmare relates to the dreamer's primary unresolved emotional concerns. Hartmann is Professor of Psychiatry at Tufts University School of Medicine and (retired) Director of the Sleep Disorders Center at Newton-Wellesley Hospital in Boston. Based on numerous studies with thousands of dreams, Hartmann concludes that dreams provide "explanatory" metaphors of the dreamer's primary emotional concerns and that they function to help make neuronal connections, not only to related emotional memories, but also to new possibilities.[3]

Hartmann's studies are reinforced by recent studies on the dreaming brain. These show that the areas of the brain that are active during REM sleep are those that process emotion and relate emotional associations to the dreamer's internal sense of self. Robert J. Hoss, author of *Dream Language*, presents concise summaries of current research in this area.[4]

In the 1980s, Candace Pert, along with other mind-body researchers, helped confirm the intricate biochemical communication network between the body and mind. Pert found that even tiny immune cells have receptors for neuropeptides, which she nicknamed the "molecules of emotion." Pert works with her own dreams. She writes, "Dreams are direct messages from your body-mind, giving you valuable information about what's going physiologically as well as emotionally."[5]

Additional research comes from the field of brain plasticity. Psychiatrist and psychoanalyst Norman Doidge, M.D., has noticed the progression of positive imagery that arises in dreams of patients in analysis. As the patient gains insight and understanding, dream imagery becomes more and more positive. Doidge sees progressions of positive imagery and positive responses within the dream as a reflection of new mapping in the brain. Positive progression is an indicator that old neuronal connections are dying and new neuronal connections are forming.[6]

MOVING THROUGH ILLNESS:
BEING WITH BIRD AND SNAKE

After surgery for ovarian cancer, Margaret began attending groups and classes at the cancer center. When she first joined the Dream Circle, she shared her nightmare about Rotting Bird and Black Snake. She told the story of how the dream had been instrumental in assuring early diagnosis and treatment. Margaret calls herself the *Nightmare Queen* because she feels that most of her insights about her own healing have come from nightmare confrontations. Margaret has found that when she works with a nightmare, it is helpful to begin with a symbol or symbols that carry the most energy. Following the steps in Chapter 3, she chooses her symbol and describes it as if for someone who has no idea what it is. Then she explores all her associations with the ten symbol appreciation questions while at the same time asking,

> What in my life feels like, or is, or was, or might be like this?
>
> Where in my life do I, or did I respond in this same way?
>
> Do I feel this experience as limiting or life-expanding?

After each exploration of a symbol, Margaret records her reflections in her dream journal:

> I'm still working with Bird. Rotting Bird is taking me way beyond the cancer and the physical implications of disease. I'm beginning to feel that Rotting Bird is also an image of my deteriorating effort to seek any kind of connection with a source of support beyond myself. I've done nothing to nurture my spiritual life since I threw in the towel several years ago trying to deal with my husband's addiction to alcohol. I think Bird is inviting me to heal my sense of broken spiritual connection.

In another journal entry, Margaret reflects on Black Snake:

> What does Snake want? Why is the snake blocking the door and what is it trying to teach me? The giant snake sparks automatic recoil. What in my life causes me to respond with such recoil? It's hard to admit, but I recoil from my own body. I've been denying that I feel damaged by the hysterectomy, but I really

feel like an essential part of me is missing. I recoil in denial of how changed I am. But there is something even stronger.

I also recognize the phallic symbolism of the snake, and I know that it's time to get some help with my aversion to sexual contact with my husband. Snake links me to my feelings of distaste about my body and sexual intimacy. How can snake help me heal?

Margaret explored the Internet and found many articles about symbols of the snake. Participants in dream circles are encouraged to explore their own associations and to look for their own metaphors before using a dream symbol dictionary or other reference sources. If participants decide to "look up" a symbol, they are encouraged to consider the author's comments in the same manner that they consider another person's "if it were my dream" comment. Dreamers are taught that one's own sense of resonance is the only measure of personal meaning. Margaret was intrigued with one of the comments she found about the snake.

Today I discovered that Snake is part of the caduceus, the symbol of the medical profession. Maybe Snake is holding together my multilayered conflicting emotions about my ability to heal. I just read that snake is considered an ancient symbol of healing. Maybe I should feel deeply touched that Snake has come to me in a dream at a time of medical crisis. But right now, I really don't feel anything but fear.[7]

GUIDED IMAGERY:
ALLOWING TRANSFORMATION

In the IASD Cancer Project, participants learn multiple, often overlapping approaches for engaging with dreams, especially nightmares. Every approach is grounded in a meditative state of consciousness. You have already learned how to breathe and relax your body. You have learned tips for remembering and recording your dreams. You have learned how to explore dream symbols with questions that bring both understanding and appreciation.

But you may want to move deeper. Symbol work usually yields intellectual understanding but sometimes fails to touch the emotional trauma of the nightmare. In the IASD Cancer Project, facilitators teach a process we call Guided Imagery for Dream Re-entry. In a relaxed, meditative state, the dreamer moves into an imaginal healing sanctuary in the presence of a supportive companion or companions. Then the dreamer re-enters the dream or nightmare with the intent to allow his or her relationship to the dream to transform. Guided imagery allows the dreamer to side-step rational thought and verbal interpretation. The process immerses the dreamer in a journey of emotional sensations and facilitates direct encounter with elements of the dream. This approach allows transformation at a sensate level.

Our guided imagery methods are influenced by the work of Belleruth Naparstek and Martin L. Rossman, M.D., who have written definitive books on guided imagery for the field of integrative healthcare.[8] Along with other imagery practitioners, they have conducted studies over the past 25 years affirming that guided meditations can transform debilitating patterns of mind, body, and spirit. Case studies and summaries of the latest research on guided imagery with people facing cancer can be found in the archives section of www.healthjourneys.com.[9] A comprehensive listing of studies can be found in anthologies of integrative oncology.[10] In her book *Invisible Heroes: Survivors of Trauma and How They Heal*, Belleruth Naparstek presents numerous case studies of those who have suffered traumas and nightmares of post-traumatic stress (PTS). She describes how the neurophysiological processes of meditative imagery affect healing with this population.[11]

From observations over the years, Cancer Project facilitators concur that guided imagery with its focus on sensate and emotional processing and its ability to circumvent verbal reasoning is also a successful approach for transforming the disturbing dreams of those facing cancer. Participants in the IASD Project repeatedly report positive changes in nightmares after practicing with the dream re-entry process. A major goal of the IASD Cancer Project is to help expand ongoing research on nightmare transformation.

PROCESS FOR DREAM RE-ENTRY

If you would like to deepen your approach to nightmare transformation through guided imagery for dream re-entry, then once again, focus on your breath and begin to relax each part of your body. Then imagine a **personal healing sanctuary** that feels completely safe and conducive for healing work. This place may be inside or outside, real or imagined. It can come from a memory or arise spontaneously from the deep wisdom of the unconscious. The important element is that you feel safe and ready to receive. Use all of your senses to experience this place to the fullest. Notice what you see, hear, smell, taste. Use your sense of touch. Especially notice the sensations you feel throughout your body. After grounding yourself in an imaginal healing sanctuary, then you can invite the presence of **supportive companionship.**

Artists, writers, and people who engage in any kind of creative expression will often speak of connection with an inspirational muse. Shamans and spiritual seekers build and nurture relationships with their guides. In most religions, there are accounts of mediators, like angels, who assist in connection with the Divine.

Guided Imagery experts talk of building relationship with supporters from the imaginal realm. Belleruth Naparstek speaks of inviting the presence of supportive allies; Martin Rossman talks about connecting with an Inner Advisor or Inner Healer. Journeying with a guide into the invisible world is a universal, archetypal experience.

In the Cancer Project, participants meet many different images of supportive entities: Jesus, Mary, Moses, the Holy Spirit; family members, both living and deceased; beloved pets, both living and deceased; friends and acquaintances, both living and deceased; and an array of mythic wisdom figures and animals, some realistic and others appearing more as animated cartoon characters. Among dreamers in our groups, Grandmother, Jesus, and childhood pets have most often stepped into the role of a supportive companion.

Some people do not "see" an image, but only sense that someone is near when they invoke support. Some simply feel an inner healing connection to powerful support. On the other hand, many long-time dreamers who regularly practice dream re-entry are able to connect with several different entities who show up at separate times. Each image is a unique energy of compassionate presence, and each image conveys support and guidance in its own particular manner.

The key to transforming a nightmare is to feel grounded in a sense of supportive energy no matter the form it might present. Once grounded, you can re-enter the nightmare and participate in transformation of your relationship to the subject of your fear.

You may want to record the following script for dream re-entry or to ask someone you trust to read it to you. A copy of this script can be found in the Appendix. You can also download it with background music from our website.[12] When you have become familiar with the steps of the practice, you may want to play your own choice of background music and conduct your own inner journey without a script. If at any time you become uncomfortable while listening, stop and open your eyes. You may find that unexpected issues and emotions arise and that you want to discontinue. Simply open your eyes and focus once more on your breathing. You are in charge of the process at all times. Please do not ever move into a meditative state while driving.

SCRIPT II: GUIDED IMAGERY FOR NIGHTMARE TRANSFORMATION

Once again, moving back into meditative space with the intention to heal your nightmare experience . . . arranging your body to allow energy to flow freely . . . closing your eyes . . . and once again moving your attention inside and connecting with your breath . . . breathing in, renewing . . . breathing out, releasing . . . moving down into deep relaxation . . . allowing your mind and your emotions to become still and quiet, like fragments in a kaleidoscope settling into a restful design . . . and with each breath relaxing, releasing, and moving deeper and deeper down, down into a centered place within . . . feeling calm, feeling peaceful . . .

Checking in with your body . . . sending the warm energy of the breath to anyplace that needs special care . . . breathing in, renewing . . . breathing out, releasing, relaxing . . . moving down, down into a deep place of balance and a sense of well-being . . . breathing . . . relaxing . . . releasing . . . imagining the free flow of life energy moving through your body, perhaps as streams of light, perhaps streams of color . . . perhaps feeling the movement of sensations . . . vibrating molecules of life energy flowing unimpeded from your head to your toes . . . from your toes to your head . . . life energy nourishing every organ, every tissue, every tiny cell . . . and while the energy flows in balance and harmony . . .

Opening your imagination, and now moving into an inner sanctuary, your own unique healing place that feels completely safe and supportive . . . a place you may have been before, or a place you are seeing for the first time . . . opening all your senses . . . looking around, listening . . . taking in the atmosphere . . . feeling a sense of safety and wellbeing in your body . . . breathing in the energy of sanctuary and healing that is all around you . . . savoring every detail of this healing space . . .

And now inviting an image of supportive presence . . . feeling your heart open as you recognize you are not alone . . . feeling totally seen, totally understood . . totally accepted by a companion or companions with you . . . opening your heart knowing that your experience is witnessed and shared . . . that you re-enter your dream in safety and with the certainty of support . . . feeling great strength and compassion with you . . .

So feeling firmly grounded in a sense of safety and support . . . slowly re-entering your dream with trust that the disturbing experience will shift and transform in a healing way . . .

First moving to a safe vantage point . . . observing the dream from a safe distance in the company of supportive presence . . . watching it from a new perspective, from a viewpoint of safety for as long as you like . . . totally present with all of your senses . . . viewing the dream with new lenses . . . watching for as long as you like . . . changing your perspective and distance from the dream as many times as you choose . . . feeling the support of whoever is with you . . .

Whenever you feel ready, you may slowly begin to interact with your dream . . . staying connected to the energy of your support . . . carefully moving into the experience only when you feel ready . . . initiating dialogue if you choose . . . staying grounded in a sense of safety . . .

Allowing the dream to move, to shift, to change . . . allowing yourself as dreamer to respond in new ways to whatever is happening . . . allowing yourself to be fully present . . . expressing new strengths, new attitudes . . . allowing both the images and the energies to flow . . . allowing the dream to become a new dream . . . allowing your new responses to transform the dream . . . allowing the new dream to touch your heart, your entire body, your mind, your spirit . . . staying with the new dream for as long as you like . . .

And when you feel ready to come back from this journey . . . turning to your supportive companion or companions . . . whoever has shared this experience with you . . . expressing gratitude . . . expressing appreciation for being with you and standing by . . .

And gathering up whatever you want to bring back from this journey . . . now slowly beginning to return to waking consciousness . . . knowing that you can return to an inner sanctuary whenever you choose . . . you can be in the company of supportive presence . . . you can re-enter your ever-transforming dream . . . you can respond and express yourself in new ways, allowing the new dream to act as good dream medicine in all the parts of your life that need healing . . .

Slowly coming back . . . beginning to move your fingers and toes . . . very slowly opening your eyes . . . now fully awake . . . ready now to record the experience . . . knowing that every time you go inward to engage in healing work . . . you nourish your body . . . you nourish your mind . . . you nourish your spirit . . .

SNAKE

Margaret used this technique with powerful results. After weeks of journaling about the snake in the doorway, Margaret decided to immerse herself in guided imagery to help resolve her fears and aversions. Margaret conducted two self-guided journeys into her dream. She relaxed into her favorite imaginal healing spot, a beach retreat from childhood. When she invited an image of Supportive Presence, her grandmother came and stood beside her to observe the snake through protection of a glass window. They waited and watched. On the second re-entry visit, as Margaret gazed steadily into the snake's eyes, she realized she felt less afraid. At that point, Margaret decided she was ready to talk to Snake.

She opened her journal, breathed and relaxed into a deep state of meditation. For the third time, Margaret re-entered her dream. Slowly she moved from behind the protective glass where she had been watching with her grandmother. She approached and stood close to Snake. As Margaret again gazed into Snake's eyes, she posed an essential question: "What have you come to teach me?" Here is part of her journal entry on that occasion:

Margaret: Okay, Snake. What have you come to teach me?

Snake: I came into your dream to shock you into discovering your own courage in the face of your fear of cancer. You have already come a long way in letting go of the fear. I want you to trust me as a healing presence that is always with you. Since ancient times I have been associated with healing and transformation. I want you to trust the part of yourself that is forever healed and whole no matter the circumstance of cancer or any other life challenge. And whenever you forget, I will come remind you.

Whatever you fear and resist will show up in your dreams as a threat. When your fear and resistance begin to diminish, you will perceive the image and energy as less threatening, and in many situations life giving.

Margaret told the Dream Circle about her dialogue with snake, saying, "Snake put me in touch with the enduring part of myself who is well and whole in spite of cancer, in spite of anxieties with my husband, or in spite of any challenge in my life. I have made a commitment to journal regularly with symbols of wisdom and support, no matter how scary they first appear. This will be hard, but I'll try."

Several months later, Margaret had a "big" dream, which she shared with the Dream Circle. Members received the dream with respect and amazement.

Golden Bird and Rainbow Snake

I'm entering a lush garden. A beautiful golden bird
and a huge rainbow snake are coming toward me
through the foliage. In the dream I know my fears
connected with Rotting Bird and Black Snake have
passed. When I wake up, I feel the new dream
mirrors and confirms my longing for connection
and my efforts to reach out for help. The new dream
brings me feelings of strength and a sense of hope.

TRANSFORMATION:
AN EVOLVING PROCESS

The transformation of nightmare imagery and energy rarely
happens in just one session. Usually transformation takes place
over time and includes ongoing re-entry sessions and dialogue.
Transformation often requires several evolving dreams, several
meditative experiences, and several waking life experiences. Emily's
example takes place over a span of three months.

Dream #1: In her nightmare Emily is attacked by a wild, snarling
dog, and she wakes in terror.

Emily engages the dream by first breathing into a meditative space
and then doing basic symbol appreciation work (Chapter 3). Because
she loves to draw, she sketches, then paints the snarling dog. She
becomes aware that "Snarling Dog" is like her own repressed anger.
Through guided imagery for dream re-entry, she dialogues with the
dog and discovers that the angry, snarling part of herself is desperate
to find a way to express itself and be listened to. She begins to keep
track of how often she feels angry and what situations trigger the
upsets.

Dream #2: A scary dog appears and stalks Emily, but does not attack.

Emily now uses the image of Stalking Dog as a focus for meditation. She dialogues with the dog and discovers it feels hungry and neglected. In meditation, she feeds it. At the end of each day, she journals about situations and people who stir up her anger. In meditation she sets an intention to open her heart, to find compassion for her own anger and for those who stir it up. Feeding Stalking Dog is at the center of her inner focus.

Dream #3: Emily watches a wobbly little puppy that doesn't seem scary at all. It bounces up and licks her hands.

In waking life Emily continues to meditate, now focusing on the experience of the puppy licking her hands. She does a quick abstract painting while imagining the feeling of the puppy licking her hands. She holds the intention of allowing her anger to transform. She also makes a commitment to herself to speak about her anger to a cousin who is a trigger for silent rage. Repressed, debilitating anger is evolving into available assertive energy.

Dream #4: Emily is now with a beautiful big white dog. They set out to-gether for a walk through a lush forest. She feels companionship and a sense of adventure. She wakes with a sense of peace. Emily draws several sketches of Companion Dog and puts one on the front of her dream journal.

The large white Companion Dog has become a supportive, healing presence, and Emily can now close her eyes, drop down into a centered place, and call upon this energy at any time. The image of Companion Dog will connect her with newly released assertive strength. Companion Dog is powerful "dream medicine" whenever she needs it.

Re-enter one of your own nightmares after grounding yourself in a healing sanctuary with Supportive Presence. When you return, write down the experience. Note any changes from the original nightmare, particularly changes in emotions, attitudes, and interactions. Transformation with guided imagery is a process, and usually the images and energies evolve slowly over several sessions. Like Emily, in each session you may notice that the relationship to the issue at the core of the nightmare is transforming. When the nightmare has become a new dream, re-enter the new experience each day with self-guided imagery and allow the new images and energies to impact your body, mind, and spirit.

If at any time you want to terminate a dream re-entry, shift attention back to your breath and move back into progressive relaxation. Work with transforming a nightmare only when you feel grounded in a place of relaxation and a sense of safety and support. Move back into progressive relaxation any time you feel unsafe.

ADDITIONAL APPROACHES

The nightmare transformation approach developed by the IASD Cancer Project is closely related to two well-known dream-work techniques, lucid dreaming and nightmare re-scripting.

LUCID DREAMING

If you are lucid dreaming, you are asleep, and yet you know you are dreaming and that you have the choice of interacting with the dream. Lucid dreamers find that when they turn and face the object of their fear in a dream, it quickly loses its frightening hold. The imagery and the energy change. Lucid dreamers can dialogue and respond while still in the dream. Their "lucid" responses transform the dream. For a few people, lucidity in the dream state occurs naturally. For most, it is a skill that requires a lot of practice.

Laura, facilitator of the dream circle, found that she was a natural lucid dreamer ten years ago when she was in treatment for breast cancer. She shares an experience from one of her recurring dreams:

I have a recurring dream in which a frightening shadowy figure creeps up behind me. When I feel its presence, I wake up soaked with sweat. When this dream occurs for the fifth time, I realize while I'm in the dream, "This is that old scary situation. I must be dreaming!" At this point, I realize I can confront my stalker. So I turn around and shout, "Stop following me!" Then I ask, "Who are you and what do you want?"

Right in front of me, a wavering image of a hideous woman in black rags slowly changes into an image of a beautiful little girl with luminous eyes. The child says, "I'm Hope. Since you got sick, you've been going away without me. You've locked me away from you. Please take me out with you when you go for your treatments and to your doctors. Please don't keep leaving me at home all by myself. I want to go with you."

Laura's lucid encounter illustrates a basic finding. When you intentionally confront images of the unconscious, they shift. Unfortunately, for most people, lucid dreaming is a hard skill to acquire. Fortunately, most dreamers can readily participate in equally amazing transformative encounters and confrontations through guided imagery for dream re-entry. We have chosen, therefore, to offer guided imagery in the Cancer Project. Both approaches are similar and very successful pathways to transformation. If you would like to read more about lucid dreaming, there are many resources.[13]

RE-SCRIPTING

Another approach similar to Guided Imagery for Dream Re-entry and yet very different is a process for simply re-scripting the nightmare. A well-known version is Imagery Rehearsal Therapy (IRT), developed by Barry Krakow, M.D., with others at the PTSD Sleep Clinic at the Maimonides Sleep Arts and Sciences Center in Albuquerque, NM. The method is an outgrowth of Stephen LaBerge's work with Lucid Dreaming. It is different from lucid dreaming in that the dreamer "re-scripts" the nightmare after waking up instead of during the nightmare. Along with other researchers, Krakow has now treated hundreds of patients, many of them combat veterans and people who have experienced extreme violence.[14] In the IASD Cancer Project, we offer the following guidelines to participants who choose to re-visit their nightmares through re-scripting instead of guided imagery:

- Re-script the nightmare into a "new dream" that focuses on transformation of your own relationship to the nightmare situation, not on transformation of other people involved in the traumatic experience.

- If the nightmare is about an actual happening, honor the facts.[15] (For example, if someone actually died, do not change this fact in re-scripting.) Allow transformation to occur through the development of your own new perspective, or the appearance of a redeeming factor such as a supportive companion who helps bring about changes in self-attitude.

- You might imagine a future event that will bring a sense of healing. The goal is to change your attitude toward the situation, to form a new relationship to your self-image, to find a sense of peace with whatever issue the nightmare is about.

- When the dream has shifted to an experience that is no longer frightening, rehearse the new dream through guided imagery at least twice a day, concentrating on integrating the impact of the new healing imagery, especially in your body.

- At some point, when it has lost its debilitating charge, go back to the original nightmare and explore the symbols that were holding the most energy. Ask, "What did this come to teach me?"

LEAKS EVERYWHERE

Rachel, the oldest member of the Dream Circle and the member most insecure about working with dream re-entry, had a nightmare she titled *Leaks Everywhere*. In her dream, water was leaking from every faucet in her house, and the rooms and hallways were turning into rising streams and rivers. She was terrified in the dream.

Rachel was afraid this dream was about the worsening of her cancer. She admitted that she had not explored her dream with symbol appreciation questions, and that she did not want to re-enter the dream. Nevertheless, Rachel trusted the group and asked if they would share their "if it were my dream" reflections.

Margaret said that if this were her dream, the rising water would be a reflection of her own escalating emotions that were about to drown her. Sam, who often teases Rachel, said jokingly that if it were his dream, he'd bring his kayak over and teach her how to use it.

Rachel laughed at Sam's light-hearted suggestion and agreed to let the group help her rescript the ending of her dream. After the group brainstormed for a while, Rachel chose Jay's suggestion that the rushing streams could be dammed up to make a beautiful, well-stocked fishing pond. Rachel had loved fishing with her grandfather when she was a pre-teen. She re-scripted her dream so that in the new dream she helped dam up the streams. Next, she climbed into a sturdy, flat-bottom boat with her grandfather on the newly-created quiet pond. They baited their hooks and began to fish.

Rachel agreed to re-enter the new dream while the Dream Circle was still in session. With her eyes closed, she reported to the group what was happening. She smiled as she and her grandfather fished in silence. All of a sudden Rachel began to weep. While the group waited, she cried for several minutes. When she finally quieted, Laura, the facilitator, asked Rachel if she would like to share what had happened.

Rachel replied softly. "Fishing with Grandfather freed my tears. I haven't cried in a long time. I feel embarrassed, but grateful."

For the next few days, with self-guided imagery, Rachel re-entered the boat on the pond with her grandfather. In subsequent dream circle meetings, Rachel found it easier to express her emotions with the group. The dream re-scripting approach helped her find a new experience that she could draw upon for solace. The quiet pond became Rachel's first healing sanctuary, and Grandfather became her first mediator of Supportive Presence.

CHILDREN'S NIGHTMARES

Cancer affects the lives of countless children directly or indirectly through family members or loved ones. Most children go through phases where nightmares are common, and if they are facing cancer, their own or the cancer of a loved one, the nightmares may be severe. If your child is experiencing nightmares, there are therapists who are trained to work with children's nightmares and there are several excellent books that can help you.[16]

You do not need to analyze what the dream might mean or how it might connect to waking life. Instead, focus on showing empathy and support for the child's feelings.

- Encourage the child to share the nightmare, drawing or painting it, or acting it out while playing. An adult who is an empathetic listener and playful companion is the key.

- Use imagination to help the child create a less disturbing ending to the dream. Encourage drawing and acting out this new dream.

- Be playful and have fun with the re-creation process. This helps the child feel supported and self-confident that he or she can face whatever "monsters" appear in dreams or waking life!

- Each night at bedtime, remind the child of some of the supportive people in his life, his "positive" dream creations, and his own brave responses.

YOUR OWN REFLECTIONS

Journey inward to discover your own sanctuary abodes. Conduct a self-guided imagery journey each day and begin to explore the safe healing places of your inner world. You may find yourself going back to the same place or you may go to a different place in each guided imagery journey. Venture into your inner world frequently with the purpose of getting to know your personal sanctuaries for healing work.

1. Become acquainted with your images of Supportive Presence. Soon you will learn more about how to talk with them. For now, practice being in the company of your unique symbols of support.

2. Re-enter a dream that is not a nightmare. Play with moving backward and forward beyond the time frame of the dream. Imagine what led up to the dream and then imagine the dream as it moves forward. Begin to experience your role as co-creator of a new dream. Enjoy!

3. Re-enter a dream and focus in on a vague symbol. Zoom in and allow this image to come into clear focus. Enjoy your new technique for clarifying images of your dreams.

4. Re-enter a nightmare in the company of an image of Supportive Presence. Just observe the experience from a safe distance. Stay grounded in a sense of safety and support. Develop your potential as a compassionate observer of your own disturbing experiences and the suffering of others.

5. When you have allowed one of your nightmares to become a new dream, write it down. Each day, re-enter this new experience with guided imagery and allow the new images and energies to impact your body, mind, and spirit.

6. Continue to explore the primary symbols of both the old nightmare and the new dream, asking, "What did you come to teach me?"

7. Keep track of the transformation of your fears. Celebrate each time you reclaim energy that was bogged down in a nightmare drama.

8. If you are a caregiver or health professional, offer to read the nightmare re-entry script to the dreamer during a meditation session. Be with the dreamer as a compassionate witness while she or he shares the evolving dream. Your primary role is to listen and be supportive presence.

5

Engaging the Shadow

Every dream character can open the door to expanded views about who you are. On at least one level of the multiple levels of dreams, every character can function to bring insight into the dreamer's unrealized potentials that through repression, neglect, or lack of opportunity, are unconscious to the ego.

Ego is the "I" we have in mind when we say, "This is who I am." Ego is our sense of conscious identity. But ego is not the whole of who we are. The parts of ourselves of which we are unaware are called *Shadow*. The shadow parts of ourselves live in the realm of the unconscious. Nevertheless, though unknown to and unclaimed by the ego, *Shadow* energies sneak into our waking lives. Our commitment to discover and to integrate unclaimed shadow energies is an important necessity in the healing process. Dream characters can be mirrors for shadow energies that need attention.

THE SHADOW FALLS

Because shadow elements are unconscious, we cannot see them directly. Jungian analyst Jutta Von Buchholtz offers a creative analogy for understanding the process of how the Shadow forms. Von Buchholtz asks you to imagine a child standing under a big tree. On the limbs of the tree are written all the perceptions, attitudes, beliefs, values, dictates, rules, and expectations that are directly or indirectly passed along from parents and society to the young child beneath the tree. For example, on a limb of one child's tree might be the rule "Always give in to what others want so you will be liked." On a limb of another child's tree might be the dictate "Healthy mind makes healthy body."

For every belief, perception, or expectation, there is an opposite. For the first child, the opposite, shadow side of giving in to what others want is standing up for herself. She will have a very hard time accessing strength for independence because it is hidden in her shadow. For the second child, the opposite of believing that healthy mind makes healthy body is the fact that people sometimes get sick no matter their good thoughts. This child may feel guilt whenever she gets sick and wonder what thoughts caused the illness.

Now imagine that each of us as a little child stands under her or his own tree. Since every limb on every tree has a shadow side, it is easy to see that a lot of shadow falls on each one of us. In the process of growing up, the opposite of every conscious perception, attitude, and belief on the tree, falls as shadow onto the child beneath. As we embrace the qualities our family and society admire, the shadows of those qualities move into our unconscious and make a home.

Since we are unaware of our shadow, each of us discovers these hidden parts of ourselves only when we see them displayed by other people or by the characters of our dreams. This process is often called "projection," as in "You are projecting your shadow onto someone else." There is, however, no willful choice or action in the process. It may be more accurate to say that our shadow simply falls on another person or dream character. Seeing the shadow in others is as natural as breathing. It is completely unwilled. Through this natural mechanism of meeting the shadow in others and in our dreams, we can recognize and learn about unknown parts of ourselves. It is inappropriate to judge the shadow as either bad or good. The shadow is simply made up of the opposites that have fallen into our unconscious.[1]

Strong and persistent emotion is the clue to the shadow's presence. Unsettling emotion swirls around in the presence of anyone who displays characteristics you have not yet acknowledged and accepted in yourself.

As we grow up we learn to make judgments. Most of us feel that many things are "good" and many are "bad." When another person or a dream character expresses an unconscious part of you that you perceive as negative, you will probably find that you feel judgmental and critical in the presence of that person or character. Depending on the degree of negative perception, you may even feel frightened or downright hostile. Most people consider qualities such as brutality, deceit, betrayal, dishonesty, and irresponsibility to be among qualities that live in the realm of "dark" shadow. Very few of us claim these characteristics as our own. Often more subtle qualities such as anger, self-doubt, even self-hatred are also relegated to the realm of "dark" shadow.

DARK SHADOW

Dark shadow often pervades our nightmares. In the Dream Circle Amy shares a recent nightmare about an old high school acquaintance:

> "This dream is called *Edna Wants to Kill Me*. I'm on a
> beach. It looks and feels like a big storm is brewing.
> It's getting darker by the minute, the wind is howling,
> and the waves are crashing louder and louder. I feel
> an urgent need to hurry back to the safety of the
> beach house, but I can't walk. My legs feel paralyzed.
> It feels like the wet sand is sucking at my feet,
> keeping me stuck. Suddenly a woman appears. She
> looks like a mad woman . . . dirty, hippy clothes, her
> wild hair blowing in the wind and a crazed look in
> her eyes. She's huge and she's breathing down my
> neck. I'm terrified. In the dream I recognize her as

an older Edna Etchington. I know that this woman wants to kill me. I feel paralyzed, the storm is almost on us, and I wake up trying to scream, but I can't."

After a second reading, Margaret asks Amy, "So again, tell us the main feelings in the dream."

Amy speaks softly. "When the dream opens, I feel happy. I love walking on the beach. As the storm brews, I feel more and more anxious. Then I'm terrified when my legs and feet become paralyzed and I realize I can't pull my feet from the wet sand and get out of the storm. Then the mad woman appears and scares me to death. I know she's crazy. Her breath feels hot on my neck."

Margaret begins to gather clarifying information. "Describe Edna Etchington."

Amy pauses before she says, "Edna went to my high school. I haven't seen her or thought about her in years. Why in the world would I dream of her now?"

"Tell us about her," Margaret says.

Amy closes her eyes as she answers, "Well, all the kids thought she was crazy. Her mother was in and out of mental hospitals. Edna looked wild and disheveled all the time. Her hair was never combed; she wore too much makeup or none at all; she dressed like a hippy; she was sloppy. Nothing she wore ever matched. She didn't have any social skills, if you know what I mean. Never seemed to know when she wasn't wanted. She interrupted, barged right into conversations. Most of all she never seemed to realize that no one wanted to be around her. I always felt embarrassed for her and a little guilty when she was around. In the dream last night I knew she would kill me. She terrified me."

Now Laura speaks to the group, "Before asking Amy to expand on her personal associations and possible insights, please offer your projections. Respond as if it is your own dream, and speak only of your own feelings. Amy will listen. After you have spoken, Amy may respond again if and how she chooses." [2]

Emily is the first to speak. "In my version of this dream, the terror I feel lets me know that this dream is very important. Nightmares wake me up to the reality that some aspect of my life is out of balance and in need of attention. Nightmares say, 'It's time for an ego perspective to change. It's time to give up a limited self-image and get a larger view. It's time to live a bigger, more inclusive life!' All my shadow figures that scare me or stir up any kind of unusually strong emotion usually turn out to have a lot to teach me. To honor this, I need to open up and ask myself what might be some aspects of Edna that might help me. Right now, I'm not sure."

"In my dream," Margaret says quickly, "I'm feeling that Edna doesn't care one whit about what other people think. I'm feeling that she marches to the beat of her own drum, wears what she pleases, says what she wants when she wants to say it. She makes no attempt to conform. She feels no guilt about letting others down. She feels no compunction to please or take care of others. She doesn't worry about being nice or good. She doesn't worry about hurting anyone's feelings.

"A while back, Edna's way of being would have felt crazy and entirely unacceptable to me; but now I want to give her the benefit of the doubt. Actually, a very similar type shadow figure confronted me in my dreams last year. When she first appeared, I thought she was frightening and crazy. She seemed a lot like Edna. At the time, my ego was clinging to an image of myself as someone who always did and said the right things, never hurt anyone's feelings, was nice and gracious no matter the circumstances."

Margaret takes a deep breath. "The dream group helped me to see that maybe my scary dream woman could help me change a one-sided image even though I was unconscious of the one-sidedness. I asked myself if any of my shadow woman's offensive characteristics reside in me too. I didn't want to admit it, but the answer was—and always is—'of course.' I too sometimes feel most ungracious and at times am insensitive and rude, especially with my husband. I hate to see this side of myself, but deep down I know I make judgments about people and cut them off. All the energies this shadow woman displayed were hidden possibilities lurking within myself. They still are."

Laura asks Margaret, "Do you feel she taught you something?"

"She taught me to own a part of myself that can put me first. Even when she's asocial, rude, or insensitive, I can have compassion for this disowned, neglected part of myself that I always tried to keep locked away. She taught me to recognize that if I would express just a tiny bit of this 'Me First' energy at appropriate times, I would be living in a much more authentic way.

"I'm grateful to her because a bit of her self-protecting energy has been the energy that has helped me learn to say 'No' whenever I've come close to sacrificing my own soul for the sake of upholding my 'nice' self-image. She has saved me from hours of unwanted volunteer work, and she's helped me learn to put caring for my soul on the front burner."

"But in my dream, I feel like Edna is about to kill me!" Amy cries.

Laura says gently, "Amy, it works best for the dreamer to listen and take notes during the projection time. You can have the floor when everybody else has finished their projections."

"All right," Amy says, looking at each member of the group. "Please go on."

Sam, who has stayed quiet until now, says, "I've learned that when I fear I'm going to die in a dream, it's usually about the death of some aspect of my ego's limited view. I find that death in my dreams is telling me I need to let go of attitudes, beliefs, perceptions or behaviors so that more inclusive and compassionate energy can come in."

Emily speaks next. "In my dream, Edna looks disheveled; her hair is never combed. She looks sloppy and is dressed like a hippy. She obviously doesn't worry about what other people think about how she looks. I guess I could use a little of that attitude. I think I've worried about how I've looked to others almost all of my life."

Rachel comments, "If this were my dream, I'd be terrified. I hate to even think about being stuck in the sand."

"In my dream, Edna barges into conversations, seems huge and is breathing down my neck. I'm wondering what in my life feels this way," Laura says.

Amy looks startled. "Laura, wait . . . Can I respond now?"

Everyone in the circle nods in assent. Amy says excitedly, "When you said *huge*, I had a huge insight! I told you before that I was doing some paintings from my dreams. Well, about three weeks ago I started a new painting on a huge canvas—almost as big as the wall. An abstract with clashing colors like nothing I've ever painted before—wild, discordant strokes of color and disjointed shapes. It was an expression of all the negative emotions I've experienced surrounding my diagnosis, surgery and chemo treatment. I'd been painting a few hours when my husband and mother came into the studio. They reacted to the painting with shock. It seemed to scare them. My husband asked me what on earth had gotten into me. Mother just stood there shaking her head at the painting and saying 'My, my, my.' I could tell they hated my new work.

"I couldn't speak," Amy continues. "I stopped painting. I haven't been out to the studio since that night." Amy closes her eyes and lowers her voice. "I've never worked on a canvas that large. I felt almost possessed to do this piece of work. I mixed colors I've never used before. And when I was painting, I felt liberated as I expressed the pain and anger and sense of loss. I cried as I smeared the paint. I felt a release and freedom and then great joy as the clashing colors and forms appeared. I was amazed to see on the canvas what felt like the emergence of perhaps my best piece of work ever. I was devastated by Mark and Mother's response."

Jay asks softly, "What does this nightmare want? What does Edna teach?"

Amy answers slowly, "In the dream I am stuck . . . paralyzed on the beach with a storm approaching and huge Edna breathing down my neck. Laura said if it were her dream, she would ask what in her life feels like that. I know what in *my* life feels like that.

"I think the nightmare wants me to know that my love of painting is like my love of walking on the beach. It's something that feeds my soul. The storm that's coming up is the inner storm of my conflict about expressing all my emotions—the negative as well as the positive. If I can find a way to express the negative as well as the positive, then my work will be much more authentic and powerful. But I'm afraid to do this.

"Maybe Edna symbolizes the epitome of someone who expresses all her feelings to the extent that most people think she's crazy. She shows me how afraid I am that anyone might think I'm crazy, much less that I'm a bit eccentric. She's breathing down my neck, reminding me I discovered how much I love putting the unexpected forms and colors onto the huge canvas. I guess Edna is offering me a little of her unique way of expressing herself so that I can expand my own way of expressing who I am. My paralysis, my feeling of being stuck, my fear is the fear of moving forward and showing my feelings and exploring a new style of painting. I fear what Mark and Mother and others will think."

Laura waits for Amy to absorb the impact of what she's just said, and then she asks, "Amy, how can you honor this dream? How can you take in the energies you need and turn your insights into expressions and responses that are creative and life-expanding?"

Amy answers quickly, "I'll go out to the studio tonight and visit the unfinished canvas. I need to be with it again and find out what it has to say. The studio is a good meditation place for me. I'll mix up the new colors again and talk to them as I put them out on the canvas. I'll talk to the part of myself who is obviously so afraid to express herself in unexpected ways. I'll call this part of myself, Sandy, since in the dream she's stuck in the sand."

As Amy looks around to every person in the circle, she says, "I would never have seen the gifts of this nightmare without you. You have all helped me gain a new perspective on Edna and to begin to understand why she's in the dream. I'm going to keep in touch with her to find out what else she can teach me. Thank you all so very much."

When seeking the "dark" shadow energies that lie dormant in your own unconscious, first remember where they came from. They are the opposite "truths" of all the positive "truths" that you inherited as a child. With this in mind, ask yourself, "Who makes me uncomfortable?" and "Whom do I really dislike?" Ask the same question about characters in your dreams. Explore which of their qualities stir your disdain, impatience and sense of superiority. Then ask yourself if the qualities you perceive as negative in the other may also be your own capacities that you have not yet completely accepted as part of the wholeness of who you are. These capabilities may be hard to see. Like Amy, you may be so caught up in your emotional reaction to the other that until you step back and reflect on your associations to the shadow figure, you may not be able to resonate with the metaphors that also describe parts of who you are— parts that you can claim and use to become whole.

Let strong, persistent emotion be your cue that you are in the presence of your own shadow.

BRIGHT SHADOW

When she was in college, Emily idolized one of her professors, an author who later won a Pulitzer Prize. During the time of Emily's chemo treatment, the author was present in two dreams; each time, Emily felt comforted and renewed. Then Emily had a third dream.

Gift of the Round Mirror

I'm sitting in my college library. Dr. Ingram walks up to me and hands me a round mirror. As I'm gazing at my face, my features slowly morph into Dr. Ingram's; then they slowly transform back into my own.

This dream was for Emily a sensate experience of recognizing and then taking back her own creative talents that she had for years projected onto the famous author.

Like Emily, you may be unaware of positive aspects of yourself—undeveloped strengths and abilities that go unnoticed and unexpressed. These, too, may have fallen into the shadow of all the "truths" that you inherited as a child. For example, if your family highly valued athletic prowess over other talents and skills, the shadows of the athletic prowess limb on your tree might include qualities like artistic and musical abilities. Von Buchholtz also points out that there are creative life energies in the depths of each of us that have been there from the beginning but have never emerged.[3] These are the energies that make up what Jung called the Self.[4] In this book when we talk about these core, creative energies, we use the names Supportive Presence and Inner Healer. So often we are unconscious of the resources within ourselves. Many people consider traits such as unusual leadership ability, exceptional creative talent, and extraordinary healing abilities as well as attitudes such as patience and compassion to be among the qualities that live in the realm of "Bright Shadow." In waking life or in your dreams, when you discover positive aspects in other people that you do not acknowledge as possibilities within yourself, you may feel an unusually strong sense of awe and admiration in the presence of the other person. To discover the "bright" shadow qualities that lie dormant in your own unconscious, ask yourself, "Who triggers so much admiration that I see them as having exceptional attributes that I feel are totally lacking in myself?" Again, let strong, persistent emotion be your cue to the presence of shadow.

HOOKS

Of course, other people actually do have qualities that are annoying, disturbing, and even despicable. Other people actually do have highly admirable qualities. These "others" become ready "hooks" for our "projections." The key to identifying a shadow capacity in yourself is the intensity and the persistence of emotion the other person or dream character arouses and the degree to which you would say if asked, "I'm absolutely nothing like that." If you truly feel "I am absolutely nothing like that," you can be sure you are looking at a shadow part of yourself. All the people, animals, and characters in dreams, at least on one level, are representatives of inner capacities that are not only in the other, but also are within the dreamer. How you relate to a dream character gives you a clue, at least on one level, about how you relate to an unconscious possibility in yourself.

WHEN SHADOW IS MORE THAN SHADOW

On one level, every dream invites you to consider any character in your dream as a "shadow" aspect of yourself and to explore the dream from the perspective of how this character symbolizes an unacknowledged part of you.[5] However, dreams are like holograms in that they contain many levels all at the same time.

On another level, a dream character that you know or know about in waking life may give you new insight into the other person's personality so that you can alter your present perception of and your attitudes and behaviors toward the other. For example, in a dream about your child, you may notice that your child has an important need that you have been overlooking in waking life.

On still another level, the dream may focus directly on which of your ways of responding to the other person need to shift so that your relationship with the other can grow or can be released. For example, in a dream about a co-worker, Rachel saw a glaring example of her habit of always acquiescing to the other's demands. The dream presents a chance to change this habit.

The night before going into surgery, Amy's mother walked into her dream.

Mother at the Door

I am going on a trip and I'm anxiously struggling
to sort clothes and fit them into my suitcase. Time
is running out, and I know I'm going to be late
for my plane. I'm desperately calling out for help.
Suddenly, Mother knocks at my door, pushes it open,
and strides purposefully into the room. Her face is
radiant and beautiful. Her demeanor is elegant. She
glows. "I've come to help," she announces, and I feel
an immediate sense that all will be well.

After recording her dream, Amy wrote in her journal:

The Mother dream feels so comforting, yet so totally
opposite from the way I usually experience the
relationship. Here I am, ready for surgery. I know I'm
anxious, but not panicked like in the dream. Well,
maybe a little bit. I've never called out for help, and
rarely do I ask Mother for anything. I've never seen
Mother look or act like she did in the dream. She was
so assertively present, and so beautiful! In the dream
I felt closely connected and soothed. What a gift of
imagery for meditation!

Not only did this dream bring supportive energy needed for surgery,
but the dream invited Amy to feel new emotions in the presence of
her mother, to notice her mother's emotions, and to notice how both
she and mother were interacting **in** the dream. These emotions and
interactions were very different from Amy's habitual feelings and
interactions.

From this dream experience, Amy expanded her understanding
of possibilities for relationship with *Mother* on multiple levels. After
much reflection, she realized she could strengthen her own inner
mothering energies and trust herself to mother her son, Tommy. She
sensed possibilities for how she might interact more interdependently

with her actual mother. She also began to reflect on how she might relate in a deeper way to the archetypal or universal mothering energies that transcend any actual mother.

ARCHETYPAL ENERGIES

Every dream character offers the same opportunities as did the mother in Amy's dream. Each character can bring insight into shadow aspects of you, the dreamer, and also offer ways to transform relationship with the character imaged in the dream. There is also opportunity to connect with archetypal energies that are at the core of every symbol. These energies are universal in much the same way that the human skeleton is universal. Each human is unique, yet each has a human skeleton. Each person has unique associations to symbols, yet there are also archetypal energies shared by all people. Several are particularly important when you are interacting with your dreams.

Babies and Children

Living in the unconscious realm of each of us are repressed and rejected issues from childhood. Dream babies and children may be inviting you to explore undeveloped potential. They can symbolize new-born, creative energies or possibilities that are developing. A child who appears in a dream, even your own child, is a symbol. Remember that every symbol has multiple meanings. Even if the image is your own child, the symbol can lead you to insights and energies about your own childhood and your own "inner" child. The symbol may also lead you to insights about the child in the dream, and it may also connect you with archetypal energies of *Child* who transcends any particular child.

Animals

Animals in dreams may teach you to recognize your instinctual, intuitive capacities. They may guide you into expanded relationship with the "animal" parts of yourself and others. Even a symbol of an animal that you have known in waking life, like a childhood pet, can help you in multiple ways. The symbol may put you in touch with your own energies that are like those of the particular dream animal. The symbol may bring insight into a particular time or place in which you knew the dream animal. The symbol may connect you with archetypal energies that transcend the particular animal and are always available for living an expanded life. In many dreams, animals function as a link between the dreamer and a healing experience.[6]

Figures of the Opposite Gender

Women in the dreams of men and men in the dreams of women can connect dreamers with special kinds of unconscious energies. Carl Jung gave these "opposite gender" energies Latin names, *Anima and Animus*, meaning *soul*. Jung observed that a basic requirement for healing and for growing into wholeness is to know and live in balance and harmony with one's own opposite gender energies.[7] Jung put anima/animus energies in a separate category from shadow energies, but for the purposes of this book, the distinction does not matter. What matters is to recognize that through "shadow" work, characters of the opposite sex both in dreams and in waking life can put you in touch with unconscious dynamics that can bring you into expanded relationship with others and with your own soul.

In ancient Chinese writings, opposite gender energies were called Yin and Yang. Yin (feminine energies) were described in part as intuition, empathy, receptivity, openness, nurturance, and appreciation. Masculine energies were described in part as logical thinking, analyzing, classifying, organizing, competing, accomplishing goals and manifesting creativity in the world. Today we know that most of the so-called feminine energies are processes of the right brain and that most of the so-called masculine energies are processes of the left brain. However we choose to think about these "opposites," a key to healing is to become conscious of all your unconscious energies and to bring them into balance.

Wisdom Figures, Teachers, and Guides

In dreams, figures of support and guidance play prominent roles. As with Margaret's snake and Amy's Edna, a figure may look and feel threatening at first, but as you pay respectful attention to imagery and its accompanying energy, transformation occurs. Do not be surprised to find that some of your most supportive figures evolve from images that first evoked negative reactions. In following chapters, we will begin to explore inner strengths through guided imagery journeys. The *Wise Old Woman*, *Wise Old Man*, *Inner Healer*, and *Inner Advisor* are just a few manifestations of the archetypal phenomenon of inner support that you will meet.

QUESTIONS TO ASK ABOUT A DREAM FIGURE

- What are the character's personality traits? Close your eyes and use your imagination. Record your reflections.

- Is your dream character, even though it may be someone you know, asking you to consider him or her as a symbol of a shadow part of yourself? Might the interaction also help you to imagine a pathway for growth in the relationship with the person in waking life?

- What might the dream character want to teach you about how you might possibly relate to yourself and others in a more creative and life-expanding way?

- How are you interacting in the dream? Is this a different way from your usual interaction in waking life?

- What functions does the character serve in the dream? Amy's mother came to offer help. What is your character's role?

- Would any of your character's personality traits or energies help you to express your own wholeness if you were able to claim and use them in a balanced way?

BALANCED WAY

What does it mean to integrate a trait or energy in a balanced way? Rachel offers an example.

An enraged woman in Rachel's dream alerted her to her own tendency toward anger and judgmental criticism. As Rachel worked hard to take responsibility for her own anger, the character showed up in a later dream as a creative, assertive business executive. Rachel's inner work to consciously channel expressions of rage in creative ways was affirmed by the character's positive assertive energy in the later dream.

It may be helpful to think of the expressions of a trait in terms of degrees between two poles. You might perceive rage as the expression of anger at one end of a pole and assertiveness at the other end of the same pole; you might see despair as the expression of grief at one end of a pole and empathy at the other. When you think of emotional and behavioral traits as being points on a continuum, it may help you become aware of the degree in which you are shifting into balance.

You may also find it helpful to choose a thought or behavior that you usually judge as negative. Then imagine a situation in which you consider that same thought or behavior from a positive perspective. When the dream circle explores this idea, Sam says, "I've got an example. A few days ago I woke up with a dream—well, really just a fragment was all I could remember." He quickly locates the page in his dream journal and reads, "A boy rises up and murders his father." Then Sam says, "After I wrote down the dream, I wrote this," and he reads, "Murder is wrong! So why have I waked up out of this dream with a sense of relief?"

"As I worked with the dream later that morning, I reminded myself that the boy and father are symbols, not literal child and parent. In meditation with the images, I began to think that the dream is showing me the energy of a young part of me now helping to 'kill' old self-limiting patterns I developed in relationship with my father. Many of my old childhood perceptions and ways of responding still drag me down. They need to transform. Murder in this dream feels like an affirming metaphor. The dream is an experience of my becoming more balanced." Sam laughs as he says, "I am so grateful I had such a horrendous dream!"

NAME YOUR CHARACTERS

Movie stars, TV personalities, celebrities of all kinds, characters from books, and countless nameless entities from who knows where populate the world of dreams. The key to allowing these shadow figures to help you is to imagine their essential characteristics, list them, and then ask, "How might a balanced amount of this character's energy help me be a more balanced and whole person?" If your character in the dream does not have a name, give him or her a name.

Clever Thief

A man who was able to sneak in and out of houses, banks, and jewelry stores with all sorts of money and valuable items showed up in Jay's dream. Jay figured out that he could use some of this character's willingness and boldness to take what he needs whenever he needs it. He named the man Clever Thief. Jay also realized that Thief is a good image of unconscious energies that are breaking in through his dreams each night. Clever Thief helped Jay modify his tendency to wait around just wishing that someone else would hand him what he thought might make a better life. Thief taught him to help himself.

Crippled Champ

A college gymnast now competing in the Olympics appeared at the edge of Rachel's dream. She was mobbed by admirers as she stood with crutches and a taped ankle signing autographs. Her presence helped Rachel recognize her own obsessive need to be like an Olympic star in everything she does. It helped her to see that perhaps others could still love her if she allowed herself to sometimes show her vulnerability. Rachel began to invite Crippled Champ into her meditations.

Hungry Child

When Emily became worried that her partner might leave, she dreamed about a frightened, hungry little girl who was about ten years old. Emily linked the dream child with a memory of being at her grandmother's house when she was ten. Emily's parents had sent her there for the entire summer while they went their separate ways in an attempt to work out their marital problems. The dream helped Emily to feel compassion for the Hungry Child part of herself and to remember and claim the love and support she received that summer from her grandmother. She also was able to remember that she survived her parents' divorce and still has good relationships with both of them. Hungry Child connected her with resilience to move through her current crisis of possible separation from her partner.

Frog Prince

When Rachel first came to the Dream Circle, she found it very difficult to look at dreams from a symbolic and metaphoric perspective. She made skeptical remarks and dismissed the "If it were my dream" comments as contrived and silly. Over time, however, she saw how meaningful everyone in the circle found the metaphoric approach, so she worked hard to understand a symbolic way of seeing. She dreamed that a frog stood up in the water, looked at her, clapped his hands, and began to dance. Rachel loved the dream but could not articulate any symbolic meaning. When Margaret commented that her first association was the fairy tale about the frog and the prince, Rachel responded, "Yes! Working with dreams sometimes feels like kissing the disgusting frog. I've worked hard to claim some of my shadow stuff. Now I see why Frog Prince is applauding me!"

Shadow figures are not always dark and scary. It is often our greatest potentials that hide in the unconscious realm. Welcome the Shadow. Dance with the Stranger in your dreams.

YOUR OWN REFLECTIONS

When a person or animal you know shows up in your dream, greet him or her as one who has come to teach you something or to bring energy that will enrich your life. Move into a meditative state of consciousness, begin to reflect and journal.

1. Describe the essential characteristics of your character. If the traits are unclear in the dream, imagine your character and write down what you perceive as essential characteristics. Write down memories the character evokes.

2. Ask yourself if there are any parts of yourself that are like your description of your character.

3. Notice how you feel in the dream, how you are interacting, and how this might be different from waking life.

4. Are your interactions life-expanding? If not, what changes in your own attitudes might be helpful?

5. Ask yourself how a quality or qualities of your character might help you if you could display this trait in a balanced way.

6. If you are a caregiver or health professional, ask your dreamer to consider the questions above. Your role is to be a compassionate listener.

6
ACTIVE IMAGINATION:
DIALOGUE INTO NEW RELATIONSHIP

In previous chapters, it has been suggested that you might talk with images of a dream. You can do this through Active Imagination, a concept developed by Carl Jung. Active Imagination is one of several techniques that define Jung's contribution to the practice of psychotherapy. It is a process of allowing the unconscious to express itself in imagery and of engaging the imagery through dialogue or through any of the expressive arts. The concept of interacting with imagery dates back to ancient times. Jung brought the practice to the attention of modern day psychotherapy. It is a primary technique in Gestalt therapy and has been used for years by clinicians and psychotherapists from various therapeutic backgrounds. Today there are many variations on the approach, but basically Active Imagination is a process of inviting an image from the unconscious into your presence, giving it a voice, and allowing the image to speak. The rationale is that imagery, particularly from dreams, carries a repository of deep wisdom from the realm of the unconscious.

In this chapter you will learn to talk not only with dream characters but also with objects and with images of your mental, emotional, or spiritual conflicts. You will learn that you can talk with your pain, your resistance, your hope, and any psycho-spiritual dynamic that influences your healing journey. You will find this imagistic and energetic approach to be a creative complement to logical problem solving. When you are talking with a dream symbol, remember that images from the unconscious can bring insight and energy for healing and that the key question to ask is "What did you come to teach me?"

SAM'S DREAM

One morning Sam woke with a dream in which a leper suddenly appears. This was the third "leper" dream since his diagnosis.

Leper Comes Again—Surprise!

I feel hemmed in as I walk down a dark narrow hallway. A beautiful woman walks toward me. She looks horrified when she sees me—turns—runs in the opposite direction. Again and again one woman after another comes toward me and rushes away. Now a guy in ragged clothes comes towards me. I know he'll run too—No—He keeps on coming.

My stomach lurches. I've never seen a leper but know for sure I'm looking at one now. Part of his arm is missing—rotted away. Most of the side of his face is gone. I try to look away. I want to run. I put up my hand to stifle a gag. My stomach churns. My eyes are closed when I hear his voice—

His tone is unexpected—deep, rich, tinged with humor. Yes—he's laughing! He's saying, "Try the Cabernet—just try the Cabernet." I stop—look at his laughing face. My fear evaporates. It's like someone has flipped a switch. Now I'm laughing.

On a Saturday morning after his second cup of coffee, Sam turned on soft meditative music, climbed into his recliner, and relaxed into a deep meditative space. In imagination, he re-entered his dream. When the leper began to laugh and speak, Sam entered into conversation. He recorded his dialogue in shorthand. Later, from his notes, he wrote the expanded version only because he wanted to share it with the dream circle. When you engage in active imagination, your transcript is for your eyes only unless you choose to share it.

DIALOGUE WITH THE LEPER

Sam: So, who are you?

Leper: Just call me Job.

Sam: Talk to me, Job.

Job: I'm the part of you who feels like a leper—a part of you who feels shunned, rejected, isolated— who also goes around rejecting and keeping others at a distance. I'm the part of you that feels like a helpless victim. Mr. Untouchable himself.

Sam: So, Job, what's your purpose or function? Why are you in my dreams? What do you want?

Job: I want your attention. We lepers can't be ignored. All through history, we've forced mankind to confront the reality of suffering. I came into your dream mainly to shake you up, to get your attention, to help you face me and to learn to embrace me so that you come to grips with the meaning of your disease and to relate to it in a different way.

Sam: This is what you like about who you are? This is what you like about being Mr. Untouchable?

Job: I told you! I like to shake people up. I like to knock them out of their comfort zone, push them off balance. I like being a hard piece of reality that isn't easy to avoid. I also like it that I've succeeded in getting you to take me seriously. I like it that you heard my sense of humor and woke up laughing. I know that when you begin to relate to me fully, you will have a much richer life. I like my role of goading you into relating to a part of yourself in a new way.

Sam: Then there has to be something that you dislike about being Job. What do you dislike about who you are and your noble purpose of shaking me into a new place? What do you dislike?

Job: I dislike being an untouchable. I dislike being shunned and rejected. I hate my feelings of isolation. I'm rotting away. I despise having leprosy. I hate this disease.

Sam: I can empathize. I know these feelings all too well. I hate my cancer. My feelings of hatred scare me. So now, what would you say, Job, is the thing you fear the most? What scares you more than anything?

Job: I fear my disintegration. I fear that because of my deterioration, I'll never find love again. I fear the loss of my manhood—my sexual competence. And I fear my own anger and bitterness.

Sam: So what would it be that you want more than anything? What in this life do you desire the most?

Job: More than anything, I want to be healed. I want to feel restored. I want to feel capable of love again . . . to make love . . .

(Here Sam found himself crying. He stopped writing. He had come to the end of the Six Questions that the dream group uses for dialogue with a symbol. The Leper had clearly stated Sam's inner conflicts about fragmentation and restoration. After a few moments Sam continued the conversation.)

Sam: Okay. You've done it, Job. You've held up a mirror to what I'm not wanting to face. My prostate cancer feels like leprosy. I'm feeling like a victim— feeling my sexual identity is rotting away. I can't get past my divorce. I'm convinced I'll never find another woman. I know the radiation is shrinking the cancer, but I'm terrified I'll be impotent . . . and incontinent . . . Why are you laughing? Laughing doesn't help.

Job: Ah. There are times when a sense of humor is the only way through. Hang in, Sam. Today you're naming some big fears that you've been pushing under the rug. Your feelings about this cancer are all tangled up with your feelings about your divorce. That's one of the reasons that in your dream I mentioned the Cabernet. I hoped the associations to that good wine would remind you of your ex-wife, Shirley. You two used to drink the very best Cabernet. Her affair with your old friend planted the first seed of doubt about your sexual worth. This is a big piece of your identity crisis. Your sense of identity is at the crux of your fear. And it's also the key to your healing . . .

Sam: What can I do, Job? What did you have in mind when you came into my dream and offered the Cabernet? What did you come to teach me?

Job: I got you to acknowledge me and to recognize the existence and power of an Inner Mr. Untouchable. I also got you to experience yourself laughing. Laughing fueled good energy for the rest of the day. I enticed you to work with associations to Cabernet. Remember your associations to Cabernet?

Sam: Yes, I remember. I associate Cabernet with the wine I bought for Shirley. What flashes into my mind immediately is the name of the wine shop, *House of Spirits*. I can feel the energy of the neon sign flashing all through my body. I realize I'm feeling a strong urge to get back to the metaphoric "House of Spirits." I want to reconnect with my old sense of passion—to reconnect with what feels like my lost spiritual life. How can I ever get back to what I've lost?

Job: You tell me . . . Come on, Sam . . . What do you need in order to be at peace with your failed marriage and the reality of your cancer?

Sam: I'm not sure what I need. I know I long to be able to love again.

Job: So hold onto these longings, Sam. Keep working with your dreams. How you relate to the characters in your dreams will keep you in touch with where you are in terms of approaching an inner balance, an inner harmony, an inner marriage. And of course, as you approach acceptance of the shadow aspects of who you are, you will also deepen your relationships with people in the outer world. Hold onto your longing and trust. Let your dreams and the dream-like experiences of the waking world guide you into knowing that you are loveable, that you can love and be loved in return. When you love yourself, you can love others. Let your dreams and dream-like experiences move you into genuine forgiveness and acceptance.

Sam: But I'm so angry!

Job: You're angry mainly because you fear you've lost who you are. You are unsure of your sexual worth because of losing your wife and having prostate cancer. Go talk again to your doctors about your fears of impotence and incontinence. One of the best ways to deal with fear is to find out all the facts and possible options.

(Sam paused, feeling both a sense of exhaustion and hope.)

Sam: Thanks for talking to me, Job. I didn't recognize the debilitating power of feeling so victimized. I want to rescue and heal my Inner Leper. Please stay close. Keep reminding me to "try the Cabernet." Today these words mean three things to me. I want to find resolution and peace about Shirley's leaving, focus on my spiritual quest, and talk about my fears with my doctors.

Job: There's a fourth thing, Sam—the most important. "Try the Cabernet" also means "Please don't forget to enjoy!"

Sam: That's the hardest one.

Job: But you laughed spontaneously in your dream. The joy can happen again. Some deep part of you knows you're truly okay. Trust the process, Sam. You can tap into this healing experience of joy again and again.

Sam: Yes. It did feel healing when my terror turned to laughter. And I know I can keep re-entering this part of the dream with guided imagery. I already can sense my feelings shifting. I feel a little lighter. I'll keep calling on you to help me. Thank you. Stay close and, Job, please keep speaking.

SIX MAGIC QUESTIONS

The six questions that Sam asked Job at the beginning of his dialogue are Six "Magic" Questions used frequently by participants in the Cancer Project to start an imaginal dialogue. They were distilled from Fritz Pearl's Gestalt method of dream work by Robert J. Hoss, who elaborates the method in his book, *Dream Language: Self-Understanding through Imagery and Color*.[1] You may make copies from an additional worksheet at the end of the book.

The dreamer addresses questions to the image; the image replies to the dreamer:

1. As the image, who or what are you? (Name and freely describe yourself and perhaps how you feel as the dream image) "I am ____ and I feel ____."

2. What is your purpose or function? "My purpose is to _____"

3. What do you like about who you are and what you do? "I like_____"

4. What do you dislike about who you are and what you do? "I dislike_____"

5. What do you fear the most? "As the image, what I fear most is_____"

6. What do you desire most? "What I want most is_____"

In the Cancer Project, participants ask one more question. *What did you come to teach me?* While an answer to this question often helps synthesize the paradoxical conflict expressed in the answers about fear and desire, do not get too caught up in needing an answer to any of these questions. Because Sam had practiced active imagination for a long time, he was able to step into the dialogue easily. If answers do not come to you, or if you feel that you are trying to make something happen, then relax, and simply try to be present in silence to the image that is with you. Open up and simply feel the energy.

MEETING THE INNER HEALER

In the following days, Sam dialogued with Job again. With each dialogue, he strengthened his relationship with his inner leper. A week later, he had a vivid dream that brought a decided shift in his perception of Job.

Receiving the Luminous Sphere

> I'm sitting in my office waiting for a client. There is a knock on the door, and then a guy pushes it open and slowly limps in. I'm mystified at the contrast between his shabby clothes and radiant face. He places what feels like a small marble in my palm. It's a small luminous glowing sphere. The warm energy from the sphere moves through my hand and penetrates throughout my body, filling my heart and mind with a sense of wellbeing. As the stranger is backing through the door, he laughs. I do not recognize his face, but I recognize that laugh. It's Job.

Sam had encountered the Inner Healer—a transformation figure who frequently shows up in dreams, myths, and waking life. Sam's healer limped into his dream. Inner healers sometimes appear to have been wounded. One of the great pioneers in integrative medicine, Rachel Naomi Remen, M.D., often comments that many of us have the capacity within us to become wounded healers. "My wound evokes your healer. Your wound evokes my healer . . . . A wound is also an opening."[2]

The Inner Healer is a reflection of Sam's outer world healing efforts and his persistent inner healing work. He is an image of the body's innate capacity to heal and grow. Meeting the Healer in the dream and receiving the numinous sphere is an example of an archetypal or universal healing encounter that transcends Sam's personal experience and is available to each of us, particularly as we seek the wisdom and support of the inner world. Healing figures appear in many guises in dreams, especially when someone is ill. The Inner Healer also appears in many forms when invited into guided imagery meditations. Martin Rossman, M.D., talks about the importance of forming a relationship with the Inner Healer throughout his book, *Fighting Cancer from Within: How to Use the Power of Your Mind for Healing.*

Swiss psychoanalyst Carl Jung identified a central organizing, unifying energy in every psyche which he called the archetype of the Self. Jung described the Self as an energetic process at work within each of us that strives to bring us to expanded consciousness of our essential nature of wholeness. This central energy strives to bring us into conscious relationship with our shadow elements, and into harmony with all of our disparate parts. Dreamers who meet the Inner Healer experience a living encounter with the encompassing, underlying energy of which Jung spoke.[3]

Sam's commitment to deepen his relationship with his Inner Leper was instrumental to his meeting the Inner Healer. Your commitment to deepen relationship with all your personally disturbing shadow figures will help you bring about healing encounters not only with personal but also with transpersonal healing energy. The Inner Healer is at the core of each of us. This healing energy of supportive presence wears many faces and appears in many guises in both dreams and guided meditations.

Using guided imagery to reach a place of meditative consciousness and practicing active imagination with personal symbols are powerful processes for opening into a felt sense of relationship with undergirding life energy.

GUIDELINES FOR ACTIVE IMAGINATION

1. Nurture attitudes of openness, respect, readiness to listen, allowing, non-judgment, and trust.

2. Create space and time where you can be uninterrupted.

3.   Relax into a meditative state of consciousness.

4.   Enter one of your inner sanctuaries and connect with a sense of support.

5.   Invite the presence of your dream symbol, and invite it to speak with you.

6.   Record the dialogue quickly using as much abbreviation as possible.

7.   Start with Six "Magic" Questions if they seem helpful. Then continue until you feel the dialogue is complete.

8.   Express appreciation to the image who has given voice to the unconscious.

9.   Honor the new insights and energies.

10. Make a commitment to integrate the insights and energies into waking life.

IMPORTANT EXCEPTION:

It is best not to practice Active Imagination with an image of a person you actually know in waking life. Inner and outer dynamics become too confused. It is too difficult to keep your relationship with the inner person separate from your relationship with the outer person. Jungian analyst Robert Johnson expands on this caution in his classic book *Inner Work: Using Dreams and Active Imagination for Personal Growth.*[4]

To gain insight from an image of a person you know in waking life, use the association technique from Chapter 5 for working with the Shadow. Make a list of the person's characteristics and then ask how these energies might be life-expanding for you if you integrate them in a balanced way and relate to them in a more creative way when you meet those energies in others.

DIALOGUE WITH A PART OF YOURSELF

You may also want to follow Amy's example. After her Edna dream, Amy dialogued with a part of herself who was stuck and frightened. She named this part of herself Sandy. Amy's dialogue with a scared Sandy part of herself proved a good way to gain additional insight from her unconscious and yet avoid the pitfalls of meditative dialogue with an actual person she had known. Amy gained insight and a deeper sense of relationship from the Six "Magic" Questions.

Amy: Who are you and how do you feel?

Sandy: My name is Sandy. I always feel frightened and helpless. I feel that I can't move forward, that I'm always stuck.

Amy: What is your purpose or function?

Sandy: My purpose is to slow you down and force you to ask for help.

Amy: What do you like about who you are and what you do?

Sandy: I like staying in one place a long time. I like not having to take risks.

Amy: What do you dislike about who you are and what you do?

Sandy: I hate being stuck and feeling trapped.

Amy: What do you fear the most?

Sandy: I'm afraid I won't be able to get where I want to go.

Amy: What do you desire most?

Sandy: What I want more than anything is to figure out where I want to go—and then to be able to move quickly in that direction.

Amy added: What do you want to teach me?

Sandy: I want you to find patience. I want you to find balance between being still and moving out. I want you to be at peace and totally present with both.

Amy expressed gratitude to Sandy, the frightened and stuck part of herself. The next time she felt stuck with her painting, she remembered Sandy's face and her plea for patience.

LET OBJECTS SPEAK TOO

Sometimes dream characters are so dramatic that they draw attention away from other elements of the dream, such as the objects in the dream. Fritz Pearls, co-founder of Gestalt therapy, taught that the objects in your dreams are aspects of youself, such as inner conflicts or fears that need to be dealt with and integrated in order for you to become a "whole" individual. Furthermore, Pearls claimed that the least human "things" in a dream are often the most alienated parts—those you most wish to distance yourself from. Some objects jump out as if screaming for attention. Others almost fade into the background. Every object in a dream can be imagined as a cloak of outer clues to reveal an energetic dynamic beneath. It is fun to play with objects and ask them to reply to the Six "Magic" Questions.

Margaret noticed a crumpled facial tissue in the center of a dinner plate in one of her recent dreams. She talked with it using the Six "Magic" Questions. In response, the tissue replied:

> I am a tissue. I feel soft and white and useful. I am always ready and waiting to help out when I'm needed.
>
> My purpose is to wipe tears and runny noses, but I can also wipe up spills and any kind of wet mess that happens.
>
> I like being helpful and comforting to those who need me.
>
> I dislike being balled up and thrown away.
>
> What I fear the most is that I will just be used and discarded.
>
> What I desire the most is to know that I am valued.

When Margaret asked, "What do you want to teach me?" the tissue replied, "I want you to be conscious of your fear of rejection so you can begin to let it go and accept how valuable you are."

Choose an object from your own dream. In imagination, become the object, and with the voice of the object, answer the Six "Magic Questions. Also state what you would like the dreamer to understand as your teaching. Write quickly. As you shift back into yourself, read the answers and underline the metaphors. Where do the metaphors apply in your waking life?

PERSONIFICATION

Just as you can dialogue with an object in a dream, so too can you talk with an emotion, mood, feeling of conflict, obsessive thought, a bodily or emotional symptom, and pain. You can do this by inviting the concern to become an image with a voice.

If you would like to talk with and learn from your conflicts and concerns, it is important to name your mental or emotional conflicts as precisely as possible. It is your own negative thought patterns, your own limiting perspectives, and your own conflicting emotions that you are seeking to transform and expand, not the problems of others. **All you can change is your own way of responding to your life.** That is not to say that other things will not transform as you change. Dreams will help you to identify what needs your attention. Recently, in her journal Amy made a list of the emotional conflicts she wanted to transform. She realized that Sandy was a good personification of her fear of being stuck. Soon she would talk with other feelings and conflicts after asking them to personify.

FROM AMY'S JOURNAL

> This is what I need to transform: my fear of pain, fear of dying, fear of being abandoned by Mark, fear of being stuck, anger at feeling vulnerable, anger at my fatigue, my feeling of isolation with old friends, my shame over neglecting Tommy, my sense of not being good enough, feeling of depression over my mother's criticism, fear of pursuing a new style with my art.

As you begin the practice of dialoguing with an emotional conflict, let Amy's example help you.

- Name your issue, concern, or conflict as precisely as possible.

- Breathe and relax. Move into one of your sanctuary abodes and invite Supportive Presence to be with you.

- Imagine your sanctuary filling with light.

- When you feel safe and relaxed, choose one of your conflicts or concerns and invite an image to appear.

- Ask the concern to personify—to become an entity with whom you can communicate. Invite it to take on a shape with color, texture and weight. Note its size. Invite the image of your concern to have a voice so that you can communicate with it.[5] When the symbol of your concern appears, it will most likely look like some kind of threatening entity. Perhaps not. Perhaps, like Sandy, it will present as a sympathetic person or animal in distress. However it presents, breathe in the strength of your Supportive Presence, turn to the image of concern, and ask the Six "Magic" Questions. It is best to write down the replies to your questions.

1. Who are you?

2. What is your purpose?

3. What do you like about who you are and what you do?

4. What do you dislike about who you are and what you do?

5. What do you most fear?

6. What do you most desire?

Add: What did you come to teach me? If the six questions do not seem appropriate, ask and say whatever feels right.

- Listen deeply. Feel the impact of the conflict between what is desired and what is feared.

- You are still in your healing sanctuary with Supportive Presence. Imagine concentrating and directing light toward your image of concern. Imagine the light becoming a beam that surrounds and penetrates the symbol.

- As your inner sanctuary is filled with intensifying light, observe any transformation of your image of concern as it is saturated with healing energy. Open your heart.

- Now imagine the light coming into your own heart. Breathe in energy of healing. Breathe out energy of compassion.

- Savor the experience for as long as you like. Express gratitude for the power of the imagination and for energies of support and healing. Thank your Supportive Presence for standing by.

- Slowly return to waking consciousness. Record your experience. Write your reflections in your journal.

- You may need to communicate with an image of pressing concern several times. Each time, you can ask for your concern to personify as an entity with whom you can communicate. You can listen to its desires and fears. You can send light to the symbol of your concern and receive light into your own heart.

- For many people, this transformation process does not require communication with words. It is more like silent communion. Be completely present to images from your deepest self; be with them in the presence of healing energy. This is the essence of this particular healing practice.

EXAMPLES FROM THE DREAM CIRCLE

When your focus is on dialogue with energies of tension, conflict and concern, your dreams will step in to offer commentary and supportive energy. Watch for shifts and changes toward healing as new imagery shows up in your dreams.

SAM

Sam and his wife were divorced before his cancer diagnosis, and Sam was unable to release the anger and disappointment he felt toward his friend who had an affair with his wife. Sam's rage was accompanied by severe chest pains that became more and more frequent. When a complete cardiac exam revealed that there were no identifiable physical causes for the chest pains, Sam decided to talk to his anger as well as to return to the cardiologist if the pains should persist.

In meditation, Sam opened his imagination, which took him to a mountain retreat where he invited Job, now the Inner Healer, to be with him. He evoked the healing image of the moonbeam that had come during his meditations with the kayak dream. After grounding himself in the supportive energy of his symbols, Sam then invited his anger to personify.

He asked his rage to take on a shape, a size, texture and color. An image arose of a fierce, steel robot whose body was a huge vise that opened wide, then closed with a loud metallic slam.

With Job beside him and the moonbeam surrounding them, Sam sat in the presence of the robot. Quietly, Sam asked the Six "Magic" Questions and added, "What do you want to teach me?"

The robot replied, "My name is Grief. My purpose is to squeeze your heart. What I like is that I have a chance to kill you. What I dislike is that your heart is always on the run. What I desire the most is to hear you scream out in grief and plead for help. What I fear is that I'll never catch you. I want to teach you to embrace your grief."

Sam listened. Then he imagined gathering up the light from his moonbeam. He directed the light toward both the fierce robot and into his own broken heart.

Sam evoked these images as a full-sensory guided imagery every day for several weeks. Very slowly, the image of the fierce robot transformed into an image of an eight-year-old boy. The child was weeping. Sam was able to claim the boy's grief as his own.

At this point, Sam had a vivid dream in which he was at a funeral. In the dream he was totally immersed in his grief, but he also could feel his own strength and gratitude. The dream marked a turning point. Slowly, as compassion grew, Sam's pains of betrayal went away. His anger toward his wife's lover no longer intruded because Grief was no longer chasing him.

JAY

Before his surgery, Jay became physically paralyzed in a nightmare that repeated several times. In Jay's recurring nightmare, he was walking down a street and suddenly was encapsulated in darkness. In the dream he felt momentarily paralyzed. When Jay re-entered the dream, he invited his sense of paralysis to become an image with whom he could dialogue. Slowly, the feeling of paralysis became an image of a large black cocoon.

In response to Jay's six questions, Cocoon replied, "I'm a cocoon. My purpose is to be a safe enclosure where metamorphosis takes place. I love that I'm a protective space where the mystery of transformation happens. I hate that change takes so long. I fear that I'll be broken open prematurely, and that will be the end of me. My greatest hope is that from my darkness, something beautiful will be born."

Jay was stunned by the wisdom of the cocoon. He told the dream circle that never before had he recognized how frightened he was of the unknown, or how much like a cocoon he has always been. He vowed he would try to remember the words of the cocoon whenever he was faced with something new.

In a dream soon after the dialogue, Jay was once again walking down a street as darkness closed in. A sign in a store window began to flash in neon colors, "Learn to Fly." In the dream, Jay laughed as he opened the door to the sky diving shop.

YOUR OWN REFLECTIONS

1. Choose a shadow figure from one of your dreams who is **not someone you actually know in waking life**. Consider having a conversation. Start with the Six "Magic" Questions. Continue the dialogue as long as you choose.

2. If you encounter an interesting inanimate object in your dream, give the object a voice. Let the image speak. Start with the Six "Magic" Questions. Also ask the object, "What do you want to teach me?" You can use Worksheet 2 in the back of the book.

3. Make a list of your specific pressing concerns. Name your fears and all the places in your life where you are holding tension.

4. You may want to dialogue with pain, an emotion, or inner conflict. Move into an inner sanctuary, invite a companion of Supportive Presence, then invite the emotion or conflict to personify, to become an image. Let the image take on a size, shape, texture, and colors. Sit in the presence of your image and feel the energy. If you choose, begin a dialogue, perhaps starting with the Six "Magic" Questions. Remember to ask what this symbol would like to teach you. For the richest experience, write down the dialogue or speak the responses with someone you trust who can write down the dialogue.

5. Begin to participate in transforming a nightmare image, a shadow image, or a symbol of conflict and concern by directing healing light around and through the image. Also direct the light into and all around your own heart. Practice consistently for several days. Keep a journal record of your experiences.

6. If you are a caregiver or health professional, you may offer to record the active imagination dialogue and be a silent, compassionate witness.

7
HEALING DREAMS

Healing refers to a felt sense of wholeness. Through many years of work with people facing cancer, we in the IASD Cancer Project have identified six major types of dreams that bring a sense of healing:

1. dreams of numinous encounter;

2. dreams of resolution and renewal;

3. dreams of guidance;

4. dreams that arise from transformed nightmares;

5. dreams that are reminders of past survival strategies;

6. dreams that correspond with spontaneous remission.

DREAMS OF NUMINOUS ENCOUNTER

Carl Jung felt that encounter with "the numinous" was the essence of the healing experience.[1] Sam's meeting with the Inner Healer, which sparked a visceral sense of wonder and awe, is a good example of what is meant by a numinous encounter. Sam's meeting was filled with potent energy. The high intensity encounter evoked a sense of being in the presence of extraordinary possibility. Sam could feel the energy of the dream throughout his body. Numinous encounter may occur in response to a person, animal, or spirit; or it may be sparked by an object such as a beautiful flower or compelling rock. Whenever or however it happens, the dreamer experiences an extraordinary quality akin to holiness or sacredness. The experience evokes a sense of awe, reverence, and wonder. It often evokes a sense of vulnerability such as the fear one feels in the presence of overwhelming power. But the fear is tempered with a sense of blessing—a sense of certainty that one is in the presence of possibility for healing.

Two weeks before her mastectomy, Amy had a numinous dream. Normal apprehension before surgery was exacerbated by the unrelenting fears expressed by her aunts and cousins. Before the dream, Amy was feeling very on edge.

White Stallion

I'm standing in a field, watching in awe as a magnificent white stallion thunders towards me. An aura of light surrounding him rivets my attention. He gallops to a halt two feet in front of me. He communicates that he wants me to climb on his back. Trembling, I exert every ounce of effort I can give to pull myself up. When finally I'm on his back, we gallop at full speed toward a narrow opening between two rocks. Breathing in rhythm with his breath, I feel I'm totally at one with the great horse. We glide through the narrow passageway. Now we're in a brightly lit meadow on the other side. I feel calm, safe, and at peace.

For the next two weeks, whenever Amy felt the beginnings of panic, she re-entered her White Stallion dream. Savoring the experience with all her senses, she relived the transforming encounter. On the day of surgery, Amy used self-guided imagery for dream re-entry and meditated with the images and sensations of two pre-surgery dreams. First she meditated with the beautiful image from her "Mother Dream" of the night before. Amy felt her mother's presence and re-experienced the feeling that all would be well. Then she re-imagined the experience of galloping on the back of the stallion through the narrow passage between the rocks to the bright meadow on the other side. Filled with the stallion's strength, she felt calm, centered, and supported. Amy believes that the dreams and dream re-entry meditations were support for her successful surgery and have helped hasten her recovery.[2]

Margaret had a similar experience. During her first round of treatment for ovarian cancer, she was given antidepressants to help with severe emotional upheavals. One night she had the following dream.

Golden Child

I'm walking alone on a beach, trying to forget my worries. Suddenly, a little girl about four years old with silky blonde hair materializes out of nowhere and comes running up to me. She is glowing with light—wonderful energy radiating from her. I am drawn to her like a magnet. I reach out to touch her. I am mesmerized by her laughing eyes.

Margaret reported to the dream circle that after the dream, a heaviness she had carried since her diagnosis lifted. Though she has continued to have emotional ups and downs, she has never again dropped back into the original deep depression. Soon after the dream, she was able to stop taking the antidepressants. Margaret often re-enters the dream with guided imagery and invites the presence of the little girl she now calls "Golden Child." With each encounter, she is energized and soothed.

Look back at your own dreams. Have you encountered an animal or child or any other being or object in whose presence you felt awe-inspiring power? Use the experience in self-guided imagery to keep the energy alive. As you deepen your relationship with the world of your dreams, stay open to the possibility of being touched by transforming, numinous energy.

DREAMS OF RESOLUTION AND RENEWAL

Some dreams bring about a sense of being healed without the dramatic element of a numinous encounter. During illness or crisis many dreams bring a sense of renewal, peace, calm, and strength. Sometimes, when the dreamer is feeling the most down or the most in need, a restorative dream will come. It is as if the deep psyche is offering a compensating experience. Dreamers report waking up with a strong sense of restored balance, with a sense of transcendence of inner conflict, or with certainty they will survive an illness or a difficult ordeal. They also report movement away from fear into a sense of hope; or movement away from isolation into a sense of connection and relationship.

After her hysterectomy, during aggressive chemotherapy treatment for her cervical cancer, Emily had two dreams that remain a focus for meditation.

Cancer is Gone

> I'm completing my last lap, and as I'm coming up
> out of the pool, someone yells that I've just won my
> event at a swimming meet. My coach walks up and
> asks why I've been absent from practice for so long. I
> answer, "Because I had cancer." In the dream, I hear
> myself speaking in the past tense, and I feel elation
> and a strong knowing that I am healed.

Breathing under Water

I'm swimming underwater and I'm running out of
breath. I'm terrified. Just as I'm about to pass out,
I put everything I have into one last upward breast
stroke. Suddenly I realize I'm still under the water
and that I can breathe. I look up and see light at the
surface. I test my breathing. Yes, I'm really breathing
underwater. I swim toward the light and even before
I wake up, I know I've survived.

Dream expert Jeremy Taylor, in his book *The Wisdom of Your
Dreams*, comments that when you are breathing underwater in a
dream, you are still, metaphorically speaking, way over your head and
are in no way trying to rise above or minimize whatever the dream
symbolizes. Moreover, Taylor sees the act of breathing underwater
as a metaphor of the dreamer's evolving personal strengths and
awareness.[4]

Indeed, at the time of this dream, Emily felt a growing determination
to live creatively with her cancer. Today, Emily continues to renew
the life-giving energies of her two water dreams by re-entering them
whenever she's doing movement meditation in yoga or qi gong classes.
Meditative movement helps integrate the energies into her body.
She finds it particularly powerful if she re-imagines the dreams when
she exercises in a swimming pool. Today, Emily is re-imagining the
dreams to help deal with her fear that Andrew might abandon their
relationship.

Look back at your dreams. Notice that when you have felt
discouraged or on the verge of drowning in overwhelming emotional
worries, your dreams may have offered a compensating experience
to bring you back into balance. As you deepen relationship with the
world of your dreams, stay open to the healing, compensating nature
of the dream process.

DREAMS OF GUIDANCE

When facing illness or crisis, when seeking a creative solution for any aspect of life, dreams point out the stuck places and give glimpses of a way through. Every dream offers some sort of guidance. Like Margaret's dream about the rotting bird, many people report dreams that warned of illness before symptoms appeared. IASD Cancer Project facilitator Rachel Norment gives many examples of warning and guidance dreams from her own journey through breast cancer in her book, *Guided by Dreams*. Other good examples of guidance through cancer can be found in *She Who Dreams*, by Wanda Burch, and in *Healing Dreams*, by Marc Ian Barasch.[5]

After her first chemotherapy treatment, Emily's dream brought imagery that would help subdue nausea, a common side effect of treatment.[6]

From Emily's Journal

During a short, restless sleep, I saw a beautiful image of a round geometric design in many shades of blue. As I gazed at it, it felt like all the fragmented, ill pieces of myself were being pulled into the center of the circle, like into a cool vortex where the nausea subsided and I settled into a feeling of peace. During the night, I intentionally recalled that dream image several times and each time staved off a bout of nausea. For the next few months, meditating with the soothing blue mandala served me well, keeping the nausea at bay during and after chemo treatments.

When Laura, facilitator of the dream circle, was told she needed radiation for her breast cancer, she rejected the recommendation because years before an aunt had been burned during a poorly administered treatment. After the following dream, Laura's feelings changed.

Stand in the Light

> I'm walking down a dark alley. Out of nowhere, I hear
> a voice that sounds authoritative but also confident
> and compassionate. I hear the words, "You must stand
> in the light;" and then I see a beautiful stream of light
> in the distance. In the dream I know immediately
> that the radiation treatment will heal me.

Laura woke up feeling calm and sure. Her fear about radiation treatment was gone. In the expressive arts class at the cancer center, she created a painting of herself standing in rays of light. She looked at the painting before each radiation treatment. She told others that she had found a mantra she could repeat throughout her treatments: "I will stand in the light. I will stand in the light." As time passed, the dream and the mantra continued to yield new depths of meaning, particularly as she sought to deepen her spiritual life.

Often dreams offer highly specific comments on decisions about treatment options and life-style changes. Earlier we mentioned Jay's dreams that influenced his decision to stop smoking. Later, Jay's dreams about losing his "voice" were a big impetus to find help with the emotional issues of becoming more assertive.

In the dream circle, Rachel reports many dreams about food. She is a bit overweight and doesn't often comply with suggestions from the nutritionist.

From Rachel's Journal

> In my dreams I sometimes see specific foods that I
> ordinarily avoid because I don't like them. But in my
> dreams these foods seem very desirable and I wake
> up craving them. I guess my body needs them. I'm
> talking mostly about green vegetables. After a veggie
> dream, I usually buy, eat and enjoy whatever was so
> enticing in the dream. Then there are lots of dreams
> where I stuff myself with fats and sweets until I feel
> ill and uncomfortable in my tight clothes. These
> dreams help me to avoid actual tasty temptations, at
> least for a short while.

My dreams also push me to exercise. So far, I've refused to go to an exercise program. Recently I've had a couple of nightmares that are urging me to do something about my out-of-shape condition. The dreams are about being on a trip with old friends. In the dreams, I'm trying to keep up with my companions, but my legs are so huge I can only waddle along. Soon my friends are out of sight, and I'm left all alone panting and collapsing like a puddle of lard. In a dream last week, a chocolate cake exploded in my face. Guess it's time to do something since the dream is so clearly in my face.

Sometimes a dream will seem to be offering a specific remedy such as a particular herb or a food. Pay attention. Be cautious. Explore the image as a metaphor and check that the remedy is not harmful.

When there is an imbalance in the body, dream imagery often portrays it by spotlighting conditions such as decay and rot, broken parts of a house, a malfunctioning car, broken machinery, sick or wounded animals, contaminated water, extreme heat or cold, lots of bugs, distorted body, parts. Many images may serve as metaphors for illness by evoking sensate response of recoil. Patricia Garfield, in her classic book *The Healing Power of Dreams*, discusses illness-related imagery as well as symbols of healing.[7] Robert J. Hoss explains that color can also indicate physical distress. Rust, dirty brown, dirty yellow, and vile green are sometimes sickness-related imagery. Red sometimes accompanies inflammation [8]

It is important to remember that every dream image is a symbol that holds multiple meanings. Dreams with disturbing images of destruction and decay warrant a physical checkup; but it is highly likely that the dream is also a metaphor for other areas of life that are out of balance and in need of repair. Most important to keep in mind is that dreams bring not only symbols of dis-ease, but also bring insight and energy for how to heal.

From Sam's Journal

Every dream I've had has shown me where I am in relationship to being a whole person. One dream shows me I'm a little off here and another shows me I'm a little off there. Each dream is like a gyroscope in the sense that it is all about coming into balance.

Since diagnosis, my dreams have put me in touch with my anger and my need to blame something or someone else for any and every trouble I have. Dreams have shown me a very needy and lonely part of myself. The unknown, disowned and neglected "shadow" parts of myself have marched out onto the stage, playing key roles in my dream dramas. I've dreamed about homeless men who stalk me, a crippled beggar boy who haunts me. Several times I've dreamed about a leper. These characters have helped me know a homeless part of myself, a beggar boy part of myself, and a leper part of myself. I've dreamed about the "judge," the "critic," the "con man," and the "priest." As I've reached out to all these splinter parts of myself through working with my dreams, I've become much more accepting and compassionate. I'm better able to embrace all my conflicting parts and relate more compassionately to similar traits in others.

Another big issue has been my relationship with women and with my own feminine energy. My anger and ambiguity toward feminine figures in my dreams has mirrored my anger and ambiguity toward my ex-wife. And my relationship with her has in large part been a mirror of my separation within myself. Dreams have helped guide me in working through the anger and moving toward acceptance and forgiveness. As I learn to relate to my own inner feminine, I hope I can find new ways to relate to the women in my life.

My dreams are trying to bring me into a more
balanced and expanded relationship with my whole
life as well as lead me into a sense of meaning
and purpose. For me, these functions are spiritual
goals. I feel I'm in dialogue with a deep underlying
process that feels like an ongoing relationship with
Spirit, or whatever you want to call the experience
of Supportive Presence and expanded consciousness
that is so much bigger than my ego.

**Look back at your own dreams and identify where each dream
might be offering guidance.**

- What might the dream be saying about your body and
how you might move toward greater health?

- How might the dream be trying to help you expand your
present beliefs and attitudes?

- How might the dream be offering new perspectives on a
past or present situation?

- How might the dream be trying to guide you to interact
in a new way?

- How might the dream be preparing you for dealing
creatively with a future situation?

- How might the dream be trying to bring you into deeper
relationship with your spiritual life?

DREAMS FROM TRANSFORMED NIGHTMARES

As you learned from examples in the chapter on nightmares,
often a healing dream arises as a culmination dream after long, hard
inner work. Nightmares are frequently the beginning point for a series

in which the final dream is a healing dream. Between each dream, the dreamer dialogues with the dream material and meditates with the imagery. Perhaps with journaling, expressive arts, or meditative movement, the dreamer participates in as many ways as possible to assist in transforming the energy. The new imagery becomes potent energy for healing the body, mind, and spirit through guided imagery.

PLAY-DOH SNAKES

Jay reports a transforming dream series about snakes. The first was a nightmare in which poisonous snakes were in every room of his house. After talking with circle members, Jay concurred that, on one level, the snakes were symbolic representations of terrible childhood fears that had been repressed through the years. After several weeks of journaling about his fears and meditating with images of the snakes, Jay had another dream with a completely different tone.

He was in his kitchen with his small son, making brightly colored snakes out of Play-Doh. They were laughing and having fun. When he woke up, he knew that he had come to a new relationship with his personal snakes. With new perspective on early fears, Jay felt free to play. Jay meditated with the Play-Doh snakes during treatments and diagnostic tests. He re-entered the Play-Doh dream when he was having stressful times with his boss or wife. The transformed snakes became imagery and energy for shifting into relaxation and play.

FORGIVING EMBRACE

Laura offers a dramatic example of transformed nightmares. For several years, she had nightmares about her father, who had died six years before her breast cancer diagnosis. As her surgery date drew near, Laura had more nightmares about her father. Using the Symbol Appreciation questions in Chapter 3, Laura worked with her nightmares at home and shared several of them with her therapist. Gradually she found courage to face her life-long feelings of frustration and rage in the relationship with her father. She found the courage to face shadow aspects of herself that had formed through relationship patterns with her father.

A few days before surgery, instead of a nightmare, Laura had a "healing" dream in which she and her father were reaching out to one another for forgiveness. In the dream they embraced. The sensations of that embrace were "realer than real," and Laura knew on waking that her entire past relationship with her father had changed.

That moment of forgiving embrace became the dream imagery Laura directed toward her long-festering father wound. Several times a day, she relaxed and re-entered the embrace with all of its sensations and emotions. She imagined that the healing energy from the dream turned into intense light; she imagined directing the light toward the place of her surgery. Doctors were amazed at how well Laura responded during the surgery and how rapidly she healed.

Ten years after the surgery, Laura continues to remember and to re-enter the experience. She feels that today she has a totally new relationship with her deceased father, and with other "father" figures. She claims new relationship with her own inner fathering energies and with the archetypal *Father*, an energy that transcends all particular fathers. Laura feels that the process of integrating her healing dream through imagery has been a prime factor in her recovery. Today she continues to re-enter the dream and soak up energy of powerful connection.

For long-term dream workers, the transformation through dreams of a relationship with someone who has died is a very common phenomenon and is always an experience of healing, reconciliation, and renewal.

Looking back at your own dreams, try to identify transformed nightmares. In what ways did the images and energies shift? As you deepen relationship with the world of your dreams, stay open to the power of nightmare transformation.

DREAMS THAT ARE REMINDERS OF PAST SURVIVAL STRATEGIES

Over and over, we emphasize the importance of noticing the feelings *in* a dream as contrasted to the feelings *about* a dream. This important distinction is easy to forget when dreams take you back to past traumas. In our long experience with cancer survivors, we have observed that often nightmares immediately following diagnosis seem to reconnect dreamers to previous traumas in their lives. These dreams usually not only stir up fear and feelings of vulnerability but also kindle the enduring strengths and coping mechanisms that brought the dreamer through. A dream that might seem nightmarish sometimes actually helps the dreamer to re-experience times of great personal resourcefulness. Dream researcher Kelly Bulkeley refers to this phenomenon throughout his book about dreams after the tragedy of 9/11, *Dreams of Healing: Transforming Nightmares into Visions of Hope.* He clearly demonstrates that nightmares can help suffering people make meaning of their experience both while asleep and awake.[9]

FINDING A ROPE

Susan was a dream circle member with ovarian cancer who moved away shortly before Amy joined the group. Susan's dreams provide a good example of trauma dreams that bring back energy of enduring strength. Years before diagnosis, Susan escaped a motel fire by letting herself down from a balcony with sheets that she had tied together. This feat required extraordinary courage and physical strength. When cancer struck, Susan dreamed about her resourcefulness three times.

Dream #1 (shortly before diagnosis): I'm trapped in a wrecked car, terrified. Then I'm escaping, holding onto thick vines as I climb down a steep embankment. I'm amazed at my strength. In the dream I say, "I can do this!"

Dream #2 (in the middle of chemo treatment): I'm caught in a burning building. Then someone hands me a rope and I'm amazed I have the strength to climb down to safety. Again, I feel in the dream, "I can do this!"

Dream #3 (during a stressful time after moving to a new town with fewer health care resources): I'm caught between sheer cliffs and feel hopelessly trapped. Then I throw a rope up and around a rock and begin to pull myself up. I feel determination and strength all through my body.

Susan commented on these dreams in a letter to Laura, "It seems that when I'm feeling down, stuck, and afraid, a dream comes to remind me of courage and strength that once saved my life. It's as if the dream hands me a rope. These dreams trigger emotional and physical strength. I'm learning I can tap into the energy with guided imagery whenever I'm feeling helpless or stuck."

Make a list of attitudes, strategies, response patterns, and resources from the past that once served you well and might again help you in moving through present or future crises. Look back at your dreams that bring up past trauma. Do they point to attitudes, strategies, or resources that might help you now or in the future? Don't forget that there is powerful energy just in the fact of surviving.

DREAMS THAT CORRELATE WITH SPONTANEOUS REMISSION

We are often asked if any members of IASD dream circles have been cured, and if there were specific dreams associated with the cure. Many of our dream circle members have passed both the five-year and ten-year survivorship markers and are still doing well. Most have accumulated several dreams that they designate as special healing dreams. All who have participated in dream circles concur that the process of dream dialogue contributes to the healing journey.[10]

Since our project began, there has been one example of a specific dream associated with a "cure." Catherine, who was in a group five years ago, suffered inflammatory breast cancer eighteen years before coming into the dream circle. This disease is often fatal. Doctors had given up hope. Catherine was prescribed palliative radiation treatment to relieve the pressure of the tumor and was moved to hospice. One Friday morning shortly after beginning palliative treatment, Catherine's doctors discovered that the cancer mass had disappeared.

This "miracle" matched a startling recent dream. Catherine had dreamed she was standing in a doorway, reaching up for something on a closet shelf. She glanced down at her breast, and saw that the cancer mass had disappeared. In the dream, just as in actuality, she knew it was Friday. In the dream she knew she was cured.

Twenty-three years later, Catherine is alive and well. She rarely speaks of her cure. On the other hand, she often makes public presentations about healing. Catherine facilitates a dream circle in a women's shelter. For her, healing is an ongoing process, an ongoing search for meaning and relationship. Other accounts of spontaneous remission, some manifested in dreams, can be found in Mark Barasch's book *The Healing Path* and in Andrew Weil's *Spontaneous Healing*.[11]

HOW DO DREAMS HEAL?

Dreams and working with dreams can bring about mental and emotional states that have been shown to correlate with physiological states associated with health. At this point in time, much research on the efficacy of mind-body practices for cancer and other illnesses is being done; however, there has been little direct research with dreams and dream work with cancer patients. Throughout this chapter, you have been offered examples of dreams and dream explorations that have brought about feelings of renewal, reconciliation, and restoration. Most dreams discussed in this book have evoked in the dreamer feelings of connection, belonging, and deep relationship. Many have helped the dreamer find a sense of meaning and purpose. Growing compassion toward self and others is frequently reported by dream circle members.

Mind-body research, much of it from the practice of mindfulness meditation, demonstrates the connection between the above-mentioned mental and emotional states and healthy physiological states. Guided imagery research also contributes to these findings. A major goal of the IASD Cancer Project is to inspire dream researchers to replicate with dream circle participants the positive studies from other integrative practices. We feel that dreams bring highly targeted imagery for the healing process, and we encourage researchers to confirm our clinical observations.

Anthologies on research from the field of integrative oncology cite countless studies that demonstrate the benefits of other mind-body practices for people with cancer. These references along with an expanded summary of the benefits of group dream work may be found at the end of this book in Appendix III.

HOW TO ASK FOR A HEALING DREAM

Since the beginning of time, dreamers have asked for healing dreams, and dreams have responded. Ruins of ancient dream temples can be found throughout Mesopotamia and Egypt, as well as throughout Greece and the Roman Empire where from the fifth century BCE to the second century CE, there were more than three hundred shrines to Asclepius, Greek God of healing. Pilgrims who sought a healing dream participated in rituals for cleansing mind, body, and spirit. Fasting, meditating, praying, and offering sacrifices, they conscientiously prepared for a sacred encounter. Temples to Asclepius gradually disintegrated, but to this day, dreamers who seek insight, guidance, and healing from their dreams cultivate attitudes similar to those employed by Asclepiad pilgrims.

Anyone can ask for a healing dream. When you are passionate about receiving wisdom and are wholehearted about acting upon the insight, you will not be disappointed.

Many dreamers regularly dialogue with the source of the dream before bedtime. Whom do you address? Find a name that resonates with your personal background and experiences. Carl Jung called the central, unifying energy of the psyche *The Self*. Members of our dream circles have suggested names that include *Dream Giver*, *Dream Maker*, *Higher Self*, *Deeper Self*, *Inner Self*, *Inner Healer*, *Inner Teacher*, *Inner Advisor*, *God*, *Goddess*, *Creator*, *Creative Spirit*, *Divine*, *Holy One*, *Holy Spirit*, *Mystery*, *Source*, *Presence*, *Universe*.

In his classic book *Guided Imagery for Self-Healing*, Martin Rossman, M.D., addresses the fact that there are many ideas about the source of inner guidance. He advises that when you receive useful guidance, be thankful and do not worry too much about where it comes from.[12]

PROCESS FOR SEEKING A HEALING DREAM

Before asking for a dream, use every effort of your conscious mind to reflect upon your concern or conflict. Journal and ask yourself questions such as:

- What may be causing and contributing to my feelings of concern and conflict?

- How do I feel about this issue?

- Do I really want resolution?

- What are some possible solutions?

- What do I not like about the solutions?

- What do I have to gain if I no longer have this concern or conflict?

- What do I have to gain if I do not find a sense of resolution or acceptance?

- What is blocking me from approaching the situation in a new way?

After you have applied every effort of the conscious mind, intentionally let go and release the concern.

- Through relaxation and guided imagery, move into a deep meditative space. Open yourself to receive insight and energy for new possibility; open to receive support for responding to the insight you receive in your dream.

- Consciously release any expectation of a particular outcome. Focus on connection with unfathomable wisdom rather than focusing on a future result.

- You might want to follow Margaret's example. Just before getting in bed, Margaret lights a candle, writes a "prayer" request in her dream journal, and imagines placing her concern in the hands of the Dream Giver.

From Margaret's Journal

Giver of Dreams: I am conflicted and concerned that I doubt my husband's ability to stay sober. Please send me a dream in which I can feel your presence and can see the concern from a larger perspective. Open my heart to trust that you are guiding me in the direction of my heart's true longing and destiny. Give me wisdom to understand the meaning you intend and the courage to respond in the way you imagine. Thank you.

- Whatever dream comes, write it down. As you journal, know that the dream is pointing to a larger perspective and deeper relationship with your concerns. You may want to ask yourself the following questions:

- What feelings are highlighted in the dream? Are they feelings that might help to bring about a more creative solution to my concern?

- What perspectives and attitudes are highlighted? Do they enhance greater possibilities?

- What behaviors are highlighted? Are they limiting or expanding my interactions?

- Does the dream want me to work with a shadow part of myself?

- Does the dream want me to work with an unresolved relationship?

- Does the dream want me to move in a new direction?

- What is the theme of the dream? How does it relate to my concern?

- What are the inner conflicts in the dream? How do they relate to my concern?

- Is the dream pointing to a completely different issue? Sometimes dreams show that there is another issue that is more pressing than the one you are focused on.

- Continue your reflections. Through journaling and meditation, express appreciation for whatever dream comes, even if you do not understand how it relates to your concern. Explore the dream through the basic Dream Appreciation questions in Chapter 3. Keep asking for clarity and insight. Appreciate that dreams come from a much larger perspective than your questions. Hold the mystery.

- Notice imagery that might reveal insight through Active Imagination. Come back for a dialogue with the image when you can.

- Look for synchronicities in waking life. These are waking experiences that feel like they are speaking to your concern or conflict. The guidance you seek will come in both sleeping dreams and waking "dream-like" experiences.

- Keep in mind that every dream comes in the service of health and wholeness. Every dream can help you to deepen your sense of relationship with yourself, others, and the source of the dream; understand and deal with conflicting feelings and moods; make creative responses in disturbing situations and relationships; respond with expanded consciousness; find a sense of wholeness.

- Stay open. Trust the process. Trust the mystery. Dream dialogue will take you deeper and deeper into relationship with the realm and source of the dream. More and more, you will experience a sense of close connection with healing energy. As you respond, all aspects of your body's healing processes are affected.

SEEKING A HEALING "WAKING" DREAM THROUGH GUIDED IMAGERY

We will focus on "waking dreams" in Chapter 9, but it is important to mention at this point that a targeted way to seek a healing dream-like experience is to use guided imagery. If you are one who feels that you do not ever remember your dreams, then guided imagery offers another way.

- Set aside at least thirty minutes of uninterrupted time for meditative dialogue.

- Breathe and relax into a deep, centered, meditative space. Progressively relax each part of your body. Notice where you are holding tension. Acknowledge where you are feeling anxious, or out of balance.

- Using all your senses, imagine being in one of your inner sanctuary abodes. Invite Supportive Presence. Savor the energies of support and new possibility that arises.

- Now, invite a "waking dream," an imaginal experience intended to bring about symbolic imagery that will bring further healing and growth.

- Give the new imagery time to develop. Using all your senses, take in whatever experience comes to you. Suspend judgment. Be fully present. Enter into dialogue with a symbol from the dream if that feels appropriate. You may want to include your Supportive Presence in the dialogue.

- Conclude your interaction as soon as you feel you have at least one clear insight to bring back.

- Whether you understand your waking dream or not, express gratitude for the power of the imagination and for the presence of support.

- Knowing that you can return whenever you choose, slowly return to waking consciousness. Record your experience. Write you reflections in your journal. Later, explore with basic Symbol Appreciation questions, symbols from your waking dream.

- Share with a supportive friend, therapist, dream circle, or guided imagery group if you have the opportunity.

- Keep seeking a healing "waking dream" until you reach a felt-experience of new direction.

SKINNY WET MOUSE AND GOLDEN EAGLE

Fear of disapproval is an emotion that repeatedly seeps into Jay's dreams. Once in a while, the dream circle will devote a session to transforming disturbing issues through guided imagery. Jay brought his fear of disapproval to one such session. Jay relaxed into his inner sanctuary. He settled into his campsite in the mountains, and invited Supportive Presence. An image of Smokey the Bear appeared. Then Jay invited an image of his fear of disapproval to come. Gradually, a skinny, wet mouse materialized. Jay placed the shivering mouse on a small circular rug between himself and Smokey the Bear. Then he invited a healing waking dream.

In the dream, Jay found himself gazing at a large field of golden wheat. He could feel a warm breeze and enjoyed the sound of the wind through the swaying stalks. In Jay's imagination, all the sensations of the experience slowly turned into streams of light. He imagined the light filling his body with the energy of well-being. He imagined the light surrounding and penetrating the mouse. Jay sat for several minutes, completely at one with the experience. Slowly, he watched the mouse transform into a golden eagle. Jay watched and felt sensations in his own body as the eagle lifted off from the field and soared away toward the sun.

Jay expressed gratitude for the experience. In his journal, he later reflected on the wet mouse, the field of golden wheat, and the soaring eagle. While he was writing about his symbols, Jay remembered a day when he was five years old. In trying to keep up with his father's long strides, Jay had tripped and fallen. Whimpering over his skinned knee, Jay heard his father's harsh retort, "Don't be such a mouse!" Transformation of the shivering mouse into the soaring eagle has become a daily focus in Jay's meditations.

MEDITATION FOR YOU

Imagine revisiting your inner wellspring . . .
breathing and relaxing into a centered place deep
within . . . standing at the rim of the wellspring . . .
gathering inner resources bubbling up as offerings
to fill your extended cup . . . watching the flow . . .
listening to the sounds . . . feeling the air on your
skin . . . opening your heart to unending possibilities
bubbling up as healing imagery before you . . . filling
your cup.

YOUR OWN REFLECTIONS

1. Look back and gather your dreams. Have you encountered an animal, child, or any other being or object that has brought you into the presence of intense, numinous power? Keep a list of imagery that triggers high intensity energy and stirs energy for new possibility. Invite numinous imagery into meditation.

2. Look back at your dreams. Notice that when you have felt defeated, your dreams may have offered a compensating experience. Keep a list of attitudes, perceptions, and behaviors in your dreams that are opposite from ones you display in waking life. Ask yourself how the compensating energy might contribute to your journey if you integrate it in a balanced way.

3. Look back at your dreams and identify where each dream is offering guidance. Is the dream

- saying something about your body and how you might move toward greater health?

- trying to help you expand your present beliefs and attitudes?

- offering new perspectives on a past or present situation?

- trying to guide you to interact in a new way?

- preparing you for dealing creatively with a future situation?

- trying to bring you into deeper relationship with your spiritual life?

4. Look back at your dreams and identify transformed nightmares. In what ways did the images and energies shift? Keep a list of transformed images. Take them into self-guided imagery to bring strength and support.

5. Look back at dreams that bring up past trauma. Do they trigger attitudes, strategies, or re-sources that might help you now or in the future? You may use Worksheet 3 in the back of this book to keep track of healing energies and your personal symbols that represent them. Use your healing symbols in self-guided imagery journeys.

6. If you are a caregiver or health professional, keep in mind the nature of guidance and healing discussed in this chapter. As you listen to another's dream with empathy and compassion, trust that your attentive listening contributes greatly to the healing power of the dream being shared.

8
Dreams About Death and Return of Cancer:
Into the Fire

More than any other dream symbol, death evokes literal interpretation and, therefore, fear. This is unfortunate, particularly for people who are facing cancer or other serious illness. The appearance of death in a dream can feel for them like an ominous warning. The view of most dream experts, however, is in accord with that of Jeremy Taylor, who says, "[I]n dreams, no matter how it appears, death is always associated with the growth of personality and character . . . . [A] dream 'death' is the necessary precursor of rebirth into 'new life.'"[1] Most dream experts say the symbol of death in dreams is an indicator of the dreamer's readiness for the death of old patterns of thinking, feeling, or behaving that no longer contribute to the dreamer's healing and growth. On at least one level of meaning, death serves as an indicator of readiness for expansion of emotional and spiritual life.

HARD SUBJECTS FOR THE DREAM CIRCLE

The dream circle has continued to meet each week except for a holiday break spanning Christmas through the second week of the New Year. Today is the first meeting after the break. As group members shed their coats and greet each other with hugs and laughter,

Rachel extends a box of homemade candy to everyone, asking them to help her get this high calorie temptation out of her house. Amy thanks everyone for the cards and flowers they sent to the hospital after her mastectomy in early December. Emily arrives a few minutes late and slips into one of the overstuffed chairs without speaking. Laura tries to catch her attention, but Emily avoids eye contact.

One by one, circle members sit down and bring out their dream journals. Jay, Sam, and Margaret place their lunches on the table. Rachel steps out to the kitchen and brings back bottled water. Laura lights a New Year's candle in the center of the table. A comfortable silence fills the room.

Laura says quietly, "I'm glad everyone was able to come today. I'm sure a lot has happened during the holidays. Please take plenty of time to check in and to introduce your dream. I remember at our last meeting Emily asked to read from her journal. We'll be sure to leave ample time for whatever she wants to share."

"I've changed my mind. I need to be here and talk, but something awful has happened, and I don't want to read my journal," Emily says, and she bursts into tears.

Laura responds quickly. "Emily, you're in a safe place here and you can say whatever you need to say. But let's begin as always with a guided relaxation into a centered place. Then we want to hear what you have to tell us." She invites the group to close their eyes, and in her soothing voice begins the opening meditation:

> "Taking a deep, slow cleansing breath . . . breathing
> in the energy of renewal . . . breathing out whatever
> needs to be let go . . . inhaling . . . exhaling . . .
> with each breath, relaxing more and more . . .
> letting go of scattered thoughts . . . allowing your
> mind to be still and clear . . . letting go scattered
> emotions . . . allowing yourself to focus only on the
> warm breath coming in . . . breath moving out . . .
> bringing renewal to all parts of the mind, body

and spirit . . . feeling release . . . mind and spirit
quieting . . . breathing in the stillness . . . relaxing . . .
moving down, down . . . centering in a deep place of
connection . . . opening to your wellspring of inner
strengths and resources . . . now opening up to the
images of your dream or dream-like experience . . .
feeling into the dream with all your senses . . .
connecting to the images and the energies . . .
opening to inner gifts you need for moving along
the healing path into this new year. Now slowly . . .
beginning to come back into the circle . . . bringing
your dream and whatever wants to be shared . . .
relaxed, centered, and connected."

The group sits quietly. Emily's head is bowed, but the other members look around the circle at each other before slowly turning towards Emily with unspoken questions and open compassion.

Almost in a whisper, Laura asks, "Emily, are you ready?"

Emily has composed herself and begins to speak slowly, quietly. "Andrew has gone. He left the day after Christmas. He said he needs to be alone with himself. Needs time to figure out what he wants to do with his life. Whether he wants to stay here or move and start all over with a new job. He said he loves me and that whatever he decides, he wants me with him."

Now Emily raises her head. Her voice is stronger as she continues. "We had some serious discussions before he left; but every time we talked, we hit a brick wall. We couldn't get past whether or not we'll get married. We've been partners for five years. Andrew was my strength through every step of the cancer saga. No one could have been more supportive.

"Andrew's the one who needs support now. He isn't happy. He thinks he might be in the wrong line of work, or that maybe he should go back to school. But if he does that, we would have to move—provided we're staying together. I can't conceive of moving!"

Emily's tears well up again. "Did you hear what I just said? I can't conceive of moving." She exhales loudly. "Damn! I can't conceive period! This is really what's at the heart of all our trouble. I can't conceive—won't ever be able to bear a child! Damn the cancer! Andrew says it doesn't matter. Of course it matters! He wants a wife who can give him children. He keeps saying I'm wrong. Keeps saying his need for time and space has nothing to do with the fact that I can't have kids."

The group waits in respectful silence. They have learned that a key to healing in any support group is that the members allow time and space for others to fully experience whatever they are wrestling with. Each member knows how unhelpful it is for someone to jump in and start making suggestions about how to fix a problem. Each knows how unhelpful it is for someone to say that everything will be just fine. After a full minute, Emily begins again.

"Andrew has gone to his brother's house. It's just an hour away, so he can still get to work easily. He doesn't have the money to rent an apartment of his own. I know he's struggling with depression, and that his problems and our problems aren't all about me. He's given and given and given in our relationship, and now it's time for me to give back. Only I can't because he's gone.

"I don't think his brother will be very much help. He's just a kid fresh out of graduate school who's working at his first job. He's ten years younger than Andrew and has a different girlfriend sleep over every weekend. And he's excited about his work and already making more money than Andrew ever made. I'm guessing Andrew will get even more depressed staying at his house."

Emily reaches for a tissue, but the box on the end table is empty. Laura takes the open box next to her chair and hands it to her. "There's love all around you here, Emily," she says. "We hope that today you'll feel fully supported. For right now, let's see how everyone is doing and what the dreams might be bringing. Will you please go first, Emily? What have your dreams been up to since we last met?"

Emily again begins to cry softly. "Being lost. Being in the dark. And then last night—this really scares me—last night I dreamed my cancer came back and I died! In the dream, I died. Somebody please help me get through this."

Laura answers quickly, "Thank you, Emily. Let's do a check in with everyone in the group, and then we'll begin with your dream. Please, everyone, share what's been happening and what your dreams have been saying. Share anything you want to share with the circle. Tell us the title of a dream, and then let's do something we don't often do. Please name a gift or guidance that you feel your dream might be trying to offer." Laura nods to Jay on her right.

CHECK IN

Jay speaks up with a strong voice. "It must be obvious to you that my thyroid surgery is healing with no damage to my voice. I'm so relieved! And Emily, I'm sorry about this hard time with Andrew. I hope everything works out for the best. My big news is that we have another contract at work and my boss has asked me to be the lead man on the job. You know about the proposal to build a new Civic Center? We got a big piece of that! We had a pretty lean Christmas at my house, but there'll be money coming in for the New Year. My wife's happy. I'm happy.

"My dreams keep after me about being more assertive. They keep reminding me that there's a wimpy part of me who lets others walk all over him. The dreams urge 'Wimpy' to speak up and speak out. The dream I brought for today has a new theme. I call the dream *Wild Ride*. What did you ask us? To name a gift from the dream? That's hard for me to do without working with it first. Let's see. In the dream I'm on this roller coaster sort of ride. I guess the gift is that I'm shown I can really enjoy the ride even though I know in advance there will be huge ups and downs. How's that?"

Everyone smiles, and even Emily congratulates Jay on his good news and quick dream insight.

Pointing to her waistline, Rachel laughs, "Well, you can see that I ate my way through the holidays. Am I ever glad they're over. I stayed away from the family events. Avoided a lot of conflict. Went out a few times with some old friends. Now that I think of it, most of my dreams were about food. But not the one I brought today. The title of this dream is *Finding Gas*—meaning gasoline for my car. I'm not sure what I think the gift is. Maybe this dream gas is a symbol for whatever it is that really fuels me. Whatever that means, in the dream my car was almost out of gas, and then I found a gas station!" Turning to Emily, she continues, "I'm so sorry you're having such a hard time, but if I can find my gas, then you can find yours, too. You know, find the fuel to keep on going!"

Sam jumps in. "I've finished the forty-five days of radiation treatment. I'm feeling tired, but well. I talked to my ex-wife, Shirley, a couple of times over the holidays and was glad to find that I could relate to her as a friend. She came over to the house right before Christmas and brought food. And wouldn't you know—she brought Cabernet. She's found another guy. Not the one she left me for, but another guy who sells insurance. This feels like a waking dream to me. What a symbol: 'a guy who sells insurance!' Maybe he'll be the security she thinks she needs. I'm so thankful I can think about her without getting torn up. I can finally let go of my hurt feelings and truly wish her well.

"I call the dream I brought today *Finding My Group*. A recurring theme for me has been that I'm lost and I'm looking for my group. In last night's dream, I'm lost again, but suddenly I come into a party. They have saved a seat for me and I know I've found my friends. They aren't people I actually know, so I feel that the gift of the dream is a sense of belonging that I don't usually feel. I hope this gift can also be yours, Emily. I hope this circle can be real support today."

Amy gets up, walks around the table, gives Emily a silent hug, then goes back to her seat. "Well," she says, "Christmas was certainly different this year. Even the first week of December there were Christmas trees in the hospital, and they were so tacky! But it wasn't all bad. Thank you again for the flowers from the group and the cards you all sent. And most of my time in the hospital was filled with caring people. I called them the Christmas Angels. Also, all my family pulled together to make the holidays good for my son. The surgery is healing slowly, and I still have some pain. Before the surgery, Laura and I wrote a script for my personal CD and she recorded it. It uses the images from a big dream that helped me choose my doctor. It has helped me a lot.

"As for the dream I brought today, the title is *Back to Grandmother's*. I could feel all through my body the gift of this one. In the dream I am a little girl sitting on my grandmother's lap. She is singing, and I can feel the softness of the blanket wrapped around us. I can smell her lavender soap; feel the vibration of her voice. The dream gift is a feeling of safety and comfort, the kind of peace I seldom feel these days."

Margaret speaks next. "Well, I'd like to borrow and use some of these gifts the rest of you have been mentioning. You just can't know how glad I am to be back! The holiday time was easier than last year, but it was still pretty rocky. As always, the holidays set off Tom's depression—and then his drinking. I stayed in close touch with his AA sponsor and went to a couple of Al-Anon meetings, so I survived. Our son and his wife came over several times with the baby, and Tom was all right whenever they were with us. I was so grateful for their visits. That baby looks just like a little elf. His name is Daniel."

As she is talking about her grandson, Margaret's face lights up. From her quilting basket she takes two newly completed squares and places them on the center table for all to see. "I hope the baby will enjoy the quilt when it's finished. He won't know how much of myself I have quilted into it, but hopefully he'll feel the energy."

As the group admires her handwork, Margaret continues. "I've written down several dreams from the holidays. The title I'll share today is *My Sister's Coat*. It's a strange dream about being with my sister in a storm. We're teenagers in the dream. I was always so jealous of her back in those teenage years. Since the dream, I've thought about phoning her. Maybe this is the gift—an urge to re-connect and mend fences. I'm sure it's also an urge to mend fences with the jealous part of myself and with parts of me that are similar to traits I don't like in my sister. In the dream I felt more compassion than I usually feel, and that's certainly a gift. Emily, I hope you can find compassion, too, for whatever parts of you need compassion as you go through all this with Andrew."

Emily looks around the circle, briefly making eye contact with each person. "Thanks, everybody. I'm sorry to be such a drag today. I knew you'd all have a lot to share after the long holiday. I knew that Amy would need to talk about her surgery. I almost didn't come because I didn't want to monopolize our time."

Laura answers firmly. "There's no better way to spend our time than on a dream about dying. The possibility of dying hovers in the face of anyone facing cancer or any other serious illness." A dream about dying is very important. We're ready to listen."

As the other members of the circle relax into the silence of meditative listening, Emily closes her eyes and breathes deeply. A few moments pass, then she opens her eyes and begins to read quietly from her journal.

Into the Fire

> In this dream it's very dark. I'm in an old house
> filled with antique furniture, but it's not any house
> I ever really knew. I'm in a room by myself holding
> a big book that's covered with dust. The book starts
> crumbling and is falling apart in my hands. On a
> torn page in big red letters, I see the word CANCER.
> Then I hear someone shouting, "Fire, Fire!" I run out
> in the yard. Several people have gathered. Everyone

seems very upset. My dog, Bullet, is running back
and forth barking. Flames are shooting up from
a small house where I lived right after I was born.
Bullet dashes into the fire. I don't hesitate for even
a second and run in after him. His coat is blazing.
I'm mesmerized as he literally goes up in flames.
His burning is so beautiful. Like a small but
breathtaking fireworks display. I'm awestruck. I'm
also sure I'm going to die in the same way, but I feel
very accepting. The dream ends with the flames
roaring all around me.

"When I wake up and remember the dream, I cry." Tears are
running down Emily's face. "Every time I think about it, I cry. Bullet
has died. I have died. And I'm afraid the dream is telling me that my
cancer is coming back."

The group remains silent for several seconds. Then Laura asks
Emily to read the dream again. After the second reading, the group
quietly and respectfully begins to ask clarifying questions.

"Is the burning house your actual first house or is it just a dream
house?" Jay asks.

"It's the actual house I lived in till I was four. It was a little one-
room cabin that my parents built on the lot where they later built a
larger house," Emily answers.

Amy asks, "You said that in the dream it's dark? Is it dark during
the entire dream?"

"Now that I think about it, it's dark inside the first house with
the crumbling book; but when I go outside to see the fire, the sun is
shining. The fire is extremely bright, and the burning dog is a bright
display of multicolored fireworks."

"Bullet is a real dog, yes?" Margaret asks.

When Emily nods "Yes," Margaret asks, "Can you tell us a little
more about him?"

Emily answers, "Bullet was a silver German shepherd who
belonged to our family from the time I was about seven until I went

off to college. He was a noble, very superior dog—loyal, intelligent, a steady companion. He was so smart I know he could have been one of those dogs who guide blind people."

"Emily, please clarify how you feel in the dream when you see the word *cancer*. And what sensations do you have when you are burning?" Amy asks.

"In the dream, I have no time to think or feel when I see the word. Someone shouts fire, and I'm immediately diverted. Action takes over. I run out. Then I follow the dog straight into the fire. It was after the dream I got scared."

"Didn't you feel pain in the fire?" Rachel asks.

"No. This dream seemed so real. I could hear the crackle, feel the heat, smell the smoke. But I didn't feel pain, and it wasn't scary. Till after the dream."

The group is quiet, each person deep into feeling the impact of the dream.

"Are there any more clarifying questions?" Laura asks. "No? Thank you, Emily for clarifying how you were feeling in the dream. Let's move on now with our projections. Remember, we're responding out of the feelings and thoughts we have when this dream is our own dream. Would someone like to begin? Yes, Sam."

PROJECTIONS

Sam says softly, "If this is my dream, I'm really struck by my feelings. In the dream, I don't feel scared. I feel awestruck. I feel accepting. These feelings are opposite from what I feel when I wake up. The dream offers big contrasts. It kind of puts me in the middle, holding the tension between opposite feelings of acceptance in the dream and fear after the dream."

Margaret picks up another thread, "If this is my dream, I'm struck by the setting. An old house with antiques. To me that possibly says something about old beliefs, old perceptions, old attitudes, old patterns of thought and behavior that are now beginning to crumble. And the little one-room cabin my parents built–it's going up in flames. In my dream, I'm looking at big-time transformation of some very old stuff, probably emotional patterns that set in before I was four years old."

"Well I'm hung up on seeing the word CANCER in big red letters," says Rachel, who is obviously upset. "I'm hung up on me dying and the dog dying. For me, the dream's a real nightmare. I have a hard time remembering to contrast the feelings in the dream to the ones I have after the dream. I have a hard time letting any dream be symbolic, especially a nightmare with cancer and dying in it. I hate this dream."

Amy changes direction, "In my dream, I felt an 'aha' when Margaret was talking about old patterns crumbling and burning. For me, crumbling and burning are strong symbols of disintegration. Whenever something dies, it makes room for something new to be born. Maybe the dream wants me to know that my fear of recurrence can transform, too."

"Before the holidays," Jay says, "when we talked about the symbol of fire in one of my dreams, we said it probably pointed to some kind of upcoming transformation. That's turned out to be true. I've had some big transformations. I'm no longer afraid of losing my voice, literally or symbolically. I'm speaking from my heart more than I ever did. If Emily's dream is my dream, then I know I'm in for big changes, probably both inside of me—like thoughts and beliefs—and outside of me—like relationships and maybe even deciding to move to a new location."

Rachel goes back to her concerns. "I hope somebody will talk about that German shepherd and Emily burning up in the fire. I really hate that image. And also talk about seeing that awful word *cancer.*"

Sam steps up to the challenge. "I will. The German shepherd is, for me, a symbol of my instinctual energies that are noble, superior, loyal, trustworthy, and intelligent—all the characteristics Emily named.

These are energies that can lead the blind—energies that can lead me out of wherever I'm blind and take me into the light of consciousness. In the dream, I don't let my fears take over. I immediately choose to follow my loyal, dependable instinctual self into the fire. I willingly choose to die in the dream. For me, this shows the possibility that I can let die any old thoughts or beliefs or expectations or patterns that are blocking me from living into the wholeness of who I am. The dream shows me I'm ready to be conscious of the old restrictive patterns from early childhood. I'm ready to let them die."

Sam hesitates before continuing. "I'm not forgetting, Rachel, that this dream has meanings on many levels. On one level it's about grieving a dog I never grieved. It's a chance to grieve any loss I never grieved. Grieving the past connects me with grief about what I fear I might lose today. It gives me a chance to grieve my cancer. The dream also shows me I can use the love and fearlessness I feel with this dog in the dream to fuel the strength and courage for facing today's challenges."

Sam adds, "As for seeing the word *cancer* in the crumbling book, I feel this shows me that cancer will no longer hold a dominant place as an emotional drain in my life. It will crumble. For me, the color red marks the importance of the word, making it highly unlikely for me not to see it. For me, the fear of cancer is crumbling. Yes. The fear is what's crumbling."

Margaret has been restless for several minutes and obviously wants to speak. "All of us here have cancer and no matter how long we live, we'll always know it could possibly come back. That's just a fact. This is a dream, and therefore, cancer is more than a fact. It's also a symbol. We've learned that all symbols hold multiple simultaneous meanings and energies for healing. For me, seeing the word *cancer* could mean that my cancer is coming back or that it's not coming back. Either way, it's important for me to decide what kind of relationship I choose to have with my cancer. In addition, seeing the word *cancer* in big red letters is a challenge to pay attention to something else in my life that cancer symbolizes. To explore this, I'd have to think of all my associations to cancer and then ask myself what in my life is like the associations."

"Will you do me a favor, Margaret?" Rachel asks. "Please make some of these associations. I'm following your train of thought and this is really helping me."

Margaret turns to Rachel and says, "Finding associations is easiest for me when I meditate and write them down, but I'll just ramble for a minute if that's helpful. For me, cancer cells are cells that go astray. They're cells that get diverted from doing what they were created to do. So I'd ask myself, 'Where in my life am I off track? Where have I been diverted from my true purpose? In what way am I not living my authentic life? Where am I not living my passion?'" Margaret pauses to think. "And then, cancer is very destructive. So I'd ask, 'Where in my life am I being destructive?' and also, 'What in my life is destructive to my healing and growth?' Then, I'd look inside and try to identify my destructive patterns. That's enough for me right now, Rachel. Does that help?"

"Thanks, Margaret. Yes," Rachel replies. "Symbolic thinking just isn't my forte. I go straight for the literal meaning every time."

Laura also looks at Rachel. "Occasionally a dream has a clear literal meaning, but because it's a dream, it also will have a lot to say symbolically. To experience the richness of a dream, we need to look at it on many levels. Does anyone else want to add to the reflections? Yes, Amy."

"Listening to the rest of you today," Amy says, "the impact of my own losses with the mastectomy hit my gut, churning up grief. I felt my fears too. But the reflections also have given me a sense of hope. I hope Emily can feel the hope too. And one more thing. Everybody's going to die. At some level I think that any death dream must be trying to prepare us for real death whenever it comes. But to me, the fire deaths in this dream don't seem literal. This feels to me like old stuff transforming into something awesome."

Laura looks around the circle and notices that Emily is animated and seems ready to speak. Laura nods and Emily begins.

"Thank you for listening so carefully, for sharing insights, and for just being here with me. When I listened to you talking about the dream as if it were yours, I was able to separate my fears that came after the dream from my decisive feelings and actions in the dream. When you were reflecting on the dog in the fire, I was able to visualize him again in a burst of fireworks, and my response was the same—awestruck—not sad or fearful. It was only later that I brought in the fear."

Emily turns to Margaret. "Your point about cancer being a symbol for being off-track, and your questions were really helpful. The one that jumped out was, *Where in my life am I being destructive?* What comes to me immediately is that I blame the cancer for all my troubles. I tell myself that the cancer made me barren and that except for the cancer, my life with Andrew would be fine. I'm avoiding taking responsibility for any part in the rift between us. I'm blaming my cancer instead of responding to the challenge of exploring our relationship and looking for ways we might save it and grow it."

She looks around the circle. "There was another question that hit home: *Where am I not living my life?* That really struck a chord. I haven't said this out loud to anyone, even to Andrew. Now I'll say it. There's something I want to do so much that it's just eating me up. I want to write a book. I want to share my journey. I want to write something that will help other women who face what I've already been through."

Emily closes her eyes. "As I tell you this, it feels just like following Bullet into the fire. My heart is pounding and I know this is something I have to do."

The group is silent, watching Emily intently. After a moment, she opens her eyes and says, "I had no idea how strongly I feel about this until now. It's like fireworks are exploding throughout my body."

Emily pauses, the corners of her mouth turning up in a half smile. "Wait a minute! How did I get into this? Andrew's gone. My heart's breaking. And I'm sitting here telling you about my hopes to write a book like an excited kid talking about a long-anticipated treat. I've become Sam's image of a person who's balancing trays of opposites."

Emily stands and extends her arms as if she's balancing heavy trays on each hand. "Here's Andrew on one side. Here's the unborn book on the other side. Both of these are eating me up. Guess that's a good description of cancer. It eats you up. But in my dream, the *cancer* word is crumbling. The old book that holds the word is crumbling. Oh please, let it be true that something new is going to be born! At this moment, I'm more excited about giving birth to a new book than I'm depressed about not giving birth to a child. This is a revelation! How can I be so excited and so depressed all at one time?

"I'll follow Bullet into the fire. I'll try to let go some old ways of being with Andrew. Maybe as I let go, he can feel free and will choose to come back. I'll ask the social worker here at the center to help me work this through. And I'll keep listening to my dreams. But whatever happens with Andrew in the future—today I'm making a commitment to my book, and I want all of you here to hold me to it."

Circle members are smiling. Laura wants to bring closure to the group before there is an outburst of comments and questions. Laura stands for the closing meditation. She has made a list of gifts from the dreams that each member brought to the session. "Our time has run out for today, she says. "Let's close and give Emily time and space to process her important insights on her own. And let's remind ourselves of the gifts we named at the beginning of the session."

Everyone in the circle stands as Laura continues, "We go from here with many gifts. Jay's dream suggests we can enjoy the ride even with its ups and downs . . . Rachel's dream reminds us we can find the gas that truly fuels us . . . Sam's dream shows that when we keep seeking, we'll find our seat at the party . . . In Amy's dream, we can sit on Grandmother's lap any time and soak in the belonging . . .

Margaret's dream reminds us we can mend fences and touch into a sense of compassion . . . Emily's dream brings to each of us gifts of unexpected possibilities and creative spirit . . . In this new year, may we allow transformation of our fears and loses . . . May we dare to follow our noble, instinctual, intuitive selves into the fire. And in a burst of fireworks, may we help bring into being whatever is trying to be born."

IF THIS WERE YOUR DREAM

- Where in your life have you felt as if you were walking into a fire?

- Is there an emotional situation in your life that feels like cancer?

- Allow Bullet to trigger a memory of a childhood pet or important animal in your life. To what energies does this memory connect you?

VISITATION DREAMS

Most cultures and schools of dream interpretation have something to say regarding dreams in which the dreamer is encountered by someone who actually died. Many dream experts agree that working with such dreams is a powerful way to participate in healing a relationship from the past.

Sometimes the dreamer feels as if the deceased in a dream is actually present. The dreamer may report that the experience feels "realer than real." Sometimes the deceased conveys assurance and comfort. Laura's dream in which she and her father embraced in forgiveness is a good example. The comforting dream visitation is always a healing experience. The instinctive response to a comforting dream is gratitude, yet too often dreamers are so shocked by the reality of the dream that they do not use the dream for ongoing healing energy. Try to remember to keep the energy alive through self-guided meditation. Re-visit the dream frequently.

Unfortunately, not all visitation dreams feel healing. Dreamers sometimes report visits from angry, vindictive, unhappy characters that feel like actual threatening confrontations. These dreams are in the category of worst nightmares. Like all nightmares, they demand attention, and like all nightmares they hold out the promise of transformation whenever the dreamer explores the symbols and energies. Work with a disturbing visitor as you would work with any shadow figure of someone you know. Write your associations and ask yourself how you might balance these qualities in your present life. Look for metaphors as you journal.

LESS INTENSE VISITORS

Some dreams about the deceased lack the hallmarks of a visitation dream. They convey neither the sense of immediacy nor a surreal quality. The deceased person is simply a small player in the dream scenario. Jay's dream is a good example.

Waving at Mike

I'm driving one of the huge earth moving machines at a construction site. My brother is standing with a group of workers on the sidelines. I wave to Mike and he waves back. I feel very confident and at ease with myself.

Jay felt that the dream confirmed his growing sense of self-esteem. Through childhood, he had revered his older brother Mike, who was killed in Desert Storm. Jay felt that the dream was more about his own inner growth than about healing a relationship with Mike, which had been close and supportive. The small exchange with Mike felt like an acknowledgment of Jay's new self-assurance.

When a person who has died is a disturbing or minor player in your dream, pay attention to how you are feeling and interacting with the person. These dreams can yield the same insights and energies for healing and growth that come from engaging with any shadow character. All come to teach, to guide, and to deepen your capacity for relationship. Ask the following questions.

- Is the interaction different from the way it was when the person was alive? What might this suggest to you?

- Is there another character who is interacting with the deceased? What part of you might be symbolized by this other character?

- What needs to transform inside of you so that you can feel compassion and peace with the deceased in your dream?

- Are there qualities symbolized by the deceased that would contribute to your wholeness if you expressed them in a balanced way?

DREAMS ABOUT DEATH OF ANOTHER PERSON

Dreams about another's death are very common and can be very upsetting. Jay shared an old dream about his son with the dream circle.

Jack Dies

In the dream, I am with my son, Jack. We are holding hands, crossing a big street with lots of traffic. All of a sudden, a giant truck careens around the corner. I try to pull us out of the way. One wheel clips Jack. I'm cradling his little body. He's dead. My heart is broken.

In the discussion that followed, Jay revealed that the dream occurred a few weeks before Jack started middle school. At first, Jay was afraid the dream was warning him about an upcoming accident, and he took every precaution to keep Jack safe. Laura commented that dreams that predict the future often occur, but even these dreams have multiple meanings. Jay reflected that with hind sight, he could see that the dream was allowing him to feel his own ambiguous feelings about the "death" of his little grade school boy who would now be a big middle school boy.

If you dream about someone dying, ask yourself:

- Is there some aspect of this person's life that is changing to which I may need to make a big adjustment?

- What belief, perception, or attitude do I need to "let die" in order to move on with this person?

- Do I perhaps need to "let die" traits within myself that I associate with this person in the dream?

DREAMS THAT PREPARE FOR ACTUAL DEATH

As Amy pointed out to Emily when they were discussing her dream about cancer and death, "Someday we are all going to die." Dreams offer insight and energy for preparing.

When the end of life is near, instead of shining a spotlight on the symbol of death, dreams seem to go into overdrive to heighten awareness of unfinished business. It is as if the deep psyche does everything possible to encourage reconciliation and restoration and to provide energy to bring about balance, peace, and a sense of wholeness. Laura told the group that for several months before she died, her mother had dreams of being re-united with people from the past. Laura also shared a dream her mother told her the night before she died.

I hear the doorbell chime. I open the door. I walk out into bright light.

Several studies from hospice settings about dreams of the terminally ill indicate that when one is actually dying, death rarely shows up as a dream symbol. Instead, dreamers who are close to death frequently report dreams of making a journey; crossing a river; going through a doorway, passageway, or tunnel; being reunited with loved ones. These dreams often contain images of the Divine, and the dreamer usually feels a strong sense of being supported.[2]

YOUR OWN REFLECTIONS

If you should have a dream about death, remind yourself that like any other dream, this dream has multiple meanings and has come to help you live your life to the fullest. Dreams of death are usually pleas to examine places where you are feeling conflict and lack of resolution. Dreams of death may be asking you to let go of something that is restricting or diminishing your sense of being who you are meant to be. If you dream about death, ask yourself:

1. Which of my beliefs, attitudes, or perceptions need to change so I can be my truest self?

2. What are my limited and limiting perceptions and ways of interacting that no longer support my healing and growth that need to die?

3. What patterns of thinking or responding are keeping me stuck and need to die?

4. What life situations and expectations do I need to let go?

5. When I let go, what new possibilities may be waiting to be born?

6. If you are a caregiver or health professional, acknowledge that you hear the feelings ex-pressed in the dream. Then you might say, "If this is my dream, I'm wondering what new possibilities are waiting to be born."

9
WAKING DREAMS:
DIVING HAWKS AND BUMPER STICKER
WISDOM

Whether you remember your dreams or not, you can always interact with a "waking" dream and find fertile material for creative inner work. You can think of a waking dream as an encounter with synchronicity. Or, you can think of a waking dream as any waking situation that you explore for its symbolic and metaphoric meaning. You can also create a waking dream with guided imagery. You can intentionally invite a meditative, imaginal experience for healing and growth.

SYNCHRONICITY

Swiss psychoanalyst Carl G. Jung was intrigued with the phenomenon of synchronicity, the phenomenon of a non-causal, yet meaningful coincidence. Jung spoke often of waking-life situations that evoke feelings of meaningful connection with inner-life dynamics. [1]

When synchronicity happens, awareness of meaningful connection seems to break into an ordinary waking moment. It is as if an event takes on expanded, dream-like implications. Jung speculated that synchronicity arises from an underlying energetic process that is constantly drawing us into expanded consciousness of connectedness. He surmised that this process is happening at all times of day and night.

Tallulah Lyons, M.Ed.

EXAMPLES OF SYNCHRONICITY
FROM THE DREAM CIRCLE

THE QUILT

Margaret experienced a startling incident of synchronicity when she decided to create a new quilt. She had planned to sew together random scraps of fabric left over from sewing projects through the years. The quilt would become a modern-day "crazy quilt" design. Her plan changed when she dreamed about a quilt made up of a design of squares with a large circle in the center of each square. In the center of each circle was a stylized, silhouette of an animal.

The day after the dream, Margaret was next door at her neighbor's house, and was stunned when she saw a square from her dream quilt hanging on the refrigerator. Only an hour before, her neighbor's fifth grader had brought home his latest creation from school. It was a blue teal circle on a red square with a silhouette of a golden flying bird in the center. The boy explained that they were learning how to use templates and stencils in his math class.

When Margaret saw the design, she felt an awesome encounter with mystery. That night, she wrote in her journal:

> When I saw a piece of the dream quilt in my
> neighbor's house, I had a sudden sense of inner-
> outer connection. On the spot, I promised myself I'd
> continue quilting together my life as both an inner
> and outer commitment to heal and grow. As I looked
> at the stenciled shape of the golden bird, I felt my
> spirit take flight.

Margaret has been working on the new quilt during weekly dream circle meetings. She says repeatedly that creating the quilt is much like developing relationship with her dreams. Both are meditative processes that feel like participation in a work of art.

SCULPTER / SURGEON

As far back as she can remember, Amy has had experiences of déjà vu, a type of synchronicity familiar to many. Perhaps you too, on occasion, have experienced something for the first time, yet have felt that you have experienced this same thing before. Sometimes Amy will be immersed in an activity she has never done before, or will be in a brand new place; yet she will feel it is familiar and has happened before. After joining the dream circle, Amy had several experiences that felt like déjà vu, yet came after a vivid dream. The most dramatic was her first-time meeting with her surgeon. When the surgeon walked into the examining room, Amy recognized him from a dream of the night before.

In the dream, Amy was with a sculptor who had created a collection of finely carved and polished stone sculptures. In the dream, she felt the power of healing energy, both from the sculptures and from the man who created them.

The next day, when her prospective surgeon turned out to look just like the sculptor in the dream, Amy was amazed. The synchronicity stirred a strong sense of reassurance. The surprising, coincidental event contributed to the meaning and mystery Amy continues to feel about her healing journey.[2]

TWO SIGNS

Jay had yet another kind of synchronistic experience. While driving home from the cancer center one day, he saw two different signs, one in front of a church and the other on a truck bumper sticker. Both said, *Speak Up!* The words resonated as a personal message. Since Jay's diagnosis with thyroid cancer, his dreams have urged him to develop a more assertive side of himself. After seeing the two signs, Jay went on the internet, located the bumper sticker, ordered it, and put it on his car. This was his gesture of conscious intent to honor the mystery of the synchronistic event.

SYMPTOMS

Sam finds that bodily responses often trigger his sense of synchronicity. As he talks with his clients, he often feels meaningful correspondence between their body language, symptoms, and an inner dynamic. When Sam developed prostate cancer, his symptoms helped put him in direct touch with his conflicting feelings about his sexual worth. Not long ago, Sam noticed periodic twinges in his heart. Last week he went for a thorough cardiology work up. Physically, everything checked out fine, so Sam will follow up with his cardiologist in six months, just to be sure. But Sam will now also focus on some heart-felt and untended emotional and spiritual issues. He is aware that he is still very conflicted about his recent divorce and cancer diagnosis.[3]

HAWKS

Emily pays attention to both her dreams and her encounters with nature as she tries to stay grounded during this insecure time of Andrew's moving out of their house. In recent weeks she has had several visits from hawks. Twice a hawk swooped down and perched on the back fence when Emily was sitting on her deck. Last week, a hawk almost flew into the windshield of her car. Yesterday when she went out for a walk, two hawks were circling overhead. Emily is not looking to the hawks for an answer to the conflicts in her life, but seeing the hawks evokes a sense of meaning and affirmation, a sense of connection to strong supportive presence. Whenever Emily meets Hawk, she feels a sense of blessing. When Emily invites Supportive Presence into her meditations, Hawk often appears.

WORDS OVERHEARD

Recently Rachel overheard a conversation at an adjacent table in a crowded restaurant. A young girl jokingly proclaimed to a friend,

"I was such a deprived child; I can now eat and drink anything I can afford to pay for!" The words hit Rachel like a targeted message. She realized that she was hearing an excuse she constantly made for her own overindulgence. She was surprised to feel that suddenly she wanted to give up her own habitual inclination to blame others, and instead, to take responsibility for her actions, particularly her addiction to food. Like all happenings of synchronicity, the words she overheard jarred Rachel into a sense of meaning and mystery.

Be on the lookout for your own encounters with synchronicity:

- In your journal, formulate the longings and questions for which your soul is seeking answers. Keep these longings and questions on the front burner of your mind. Your dreams will respond, and also there will be experiences in the waking world that will speak to you. Be ready to encounter synchronicity, the coincidental, dream-like feelings of connection and meaning that pop into waking life.

- Record your meaningful coincidences: events that are totally unexpected—events that surprise you, upset you, and frustrate you—events that knock you off balance but feel as though they are related to inner issues. Use basic dream-appreciation questions to engage at a symbolic and metaphoric level with these seeming coincidental, yet meaningful waking events.

- Ask the key question: "As a metaphor, what does this experience teach me about possibilities for moving into an expanded, richer life?"

- Be appreciative when an outer-life experience feels as if it is a response to something you are carrying in your heart.

- Be appreciative of experiences of déjà vu wherein you feel familiarity and yet know that you are in a brand new situation.

- Allow experiences in nature to speak to you. What might a cherry tree in your yard be saying about one of your soul's burning issues? Look closely at a special rock that might catch your attention. What wisdom might it offer? Note the whispers of birds and trees as you walk with the intention to listen.

- Pay close attention to unexpected emotions and the murmurings of your body. If tears spring up unexpectedly, perhaps when watching a commercial on TV, explore to see if there is a deeper issue you may have been trying to hold at bay. If you suddenly have a backache, explore the heavy burdens of your inner life before you automatically swallow a pain pill. Allow your emotions and your body to speak symbolically as well as literally.

- Find deeper meaning in spoken and written words. When you consciously carry an issue on your heart, you might get sudden insight from a piece of text, from a bill board sign, from TV, or like Rachel, from overhearing meaningful comments in passing conversations.

ORACLES

Throughout the ages, seekers have found meaningful input from randomly selected words and signs. Some people look to the Bible in this manner, opening and reading a random verse to find wisdom for a particular concern. The *I-Ching*, or *Book of Changes*, with Chinese origins dating back more than 5,000 years, is another source of ancient wisdom. For centuries seekers have looked to this book to discern synchronistic answers to important concerns.[4]

Today's market offers many modern-day "oracles" for "playing" with synchronicity—Angel Cards, Soul Cards, Animal Cards, etc. If you enjoy "synchronicity games," then join in with the assurance that your own deep wisdom can be triggered by a card that you randomly select, by a word you randomly point to, or by some other outside stimulus. Anything may stir a sense of synchronistic resonance. Also remember that you are engaging with symbols, and that all symbols carry simultaneous multiple meanings. Rarely do dreams or synchronicities convey definitive answers. Both, however, convey multiple insights. Remember that insight always comes from within, and you will either resonate with the symbol or not. Most important, remember that you are solely responsible for how you do or do not take action in response to a synchronistic encounter.

WAKING EVENTS EXPLORED AS A DREAM

Synchronicities are waking events that immediately feel symbolically meaningful, but any waking event can feel meaningful and yield dream wisdom when it is explored as if it is a dream. The dream appreciation approach is a way to step into a more objective perspective and to let go of expectations for a certain outcome. The approach is particularly fruitful whenever you might be wondering, "Why is this happening to me?" or "Why does this keep happening to me?" Instead, you can shift into dream appreciation mode and ask, "How does this waking dream bring insight and energy to help me heal and grow?" or "What does this dream want?"

The next time you experience a crisis or surprise in waking life, or a situation that keeps repeating, write it down in the present tense. Look for the metaphors. Then engage with the elements as if they are symbols from a dream. Write down your associations. Formulate dream appreciation questions as if the event is a way to clarify how you might respond in a more creative way. Look at each element of the experience as a possible metaphoric comment on an aspect of your life. Ask yourself if any of the metaphors you have used to describe the event resonate with your inner life?

DEAD BATTERY

One day Laura had an unpleasant surprise. Later, she explored the event as if it were a dream. She wrote down the event in the present tense, so that she could feel the immediacy of the emotions.

> I am rushing for an appointment, and when I go into the garage to start my car, the battery is dead. I feel dread and panic about being late.

Then Laura composed her dream-appreciation questions:

For what is this disturbing event a good metaphor?

Where do I feel that my battery has died, that my energy is sapped, that I can't get started again?

Where do I feel I'm running out of time; that I can't meet my deadline?

What helps me to recharge? How and where can I find the resources to recharge?

Where in my life do I need to stop and slow down? Where and why am I feeling the need to rush?

Why am I feeling dread and panic over being late? What does this "dream" want to teach me?

Where do I need to shift my perceptions, attitudes, beliefs, or behaviors so that I can take this kind of unexpected interruption in stride?

Zoë Newman, MFT, who lives and practices in Berkley, California, is a facilitator in the IASD Cancer Project. She has written an exciting, comprehensive book, *Lucid Waking: Using Dreamwork Principles to Transform your Everyday Life,* which offers techniques for engaging waking life with increased lucidity and a deeper sense of meaning.[5]

Newman encourages readers to examine, in the ways discussed above, not only synchronicities and everyday events as if they are dreams, but also to examine conflicts in personal relationships as if the other person is a dream figure—a shadow aspect of the dreamer. She encourages you to think of the other person who stirs up your emotions as the face of energy that can possibly connect you with a part of yourself that needs to be recognized and integrated. She asks you to view the relationship conflict from the perspective that such "waking" dreams, just as night dreams, can be in the service of healing and wholeness, and that shadow figures can serve as teachers and guides. *Lucid Waking* suggests you ask yourself the same questions you ask when you meet a shadow figure in a sleeping dream:

- Which qualities in this person disturb me the most?

- How might this person reflect a part of me? How am I like or not like . . . ? In what ways do I . . . ?

- Does this person hold a quality that could be a helpful resource if I could integrate the quality in a balanced way?

- Is this person telling or showing me something important I need to know?

- What new attitude or response pattern do I need to develop to be at peace with this disturbing person in outer life and also with this conflicting part of myself? [6]

Newman uses the metaphor of bringing a dream work "lens" to everyday life. This lens allows you to shift below surface perception and perceive the dimension of symbolic and metaphoric meaning. Instead of questioning why a situation is as it is, or why something is happening to you, you can begin to seek clarity about your own responses. Imagine that you are putting on your "dream lenses." Today, when your emotions get stirred in an encounter with some other person, write down what is happening as if it is a dream. Use the present tense. Reflect on your "shadow figure" with the above questions, asking yourself how this "dream" character might serve as teacher and guide to help you respond to life in a deeper way. Be sure to notice if the relationship might reflect an aspect of your relationship to yourself.

NO SHOWS

After Margaret's grandson was born, her daughter-in-law called many evenings to ask if she could drop the baby off for just a little while the next morning so that she could do errands. Several times Margaret juggled previous plans so that she could be available to babysit. Four times last month, mother and baby never showed up, and not until late afternoon did the mother call to explain that her plans had changed. With each "no show," Margaret was terribly disappointed and also angry at her daughter-in-law's disregard for her time and plans. With past experience of looking at waking frustrations as frustrating dreams, Margaret wrote down the situation as if describing a dream and formulated dream appreciation questions:

Where in my life am I a "no show"?

Where do I make myself a promise and then neglect to follow through?

Is there a part of myself that I am slighting, whose time I disrespect?

Where am I a "no show" with others? When am I not fully present?

When and where am I disrespectful of my own time and that of the others?

As she reflected on these questions in her journal, Margaret began to relate to the situation with her daughter-in-law with feelings of less blame and disappointment. After claiming her own capacity for not showing up for herself and for others, she was better able to feel compassion for her over-stressed daughter-in-law and to come up with a plan for calling to double check the requested times. Margaret also reflected on another question: Might there ever be a time when my being a "no show" could be a healing response?

It occurred to Margaret that maybe it would be healthy to set clearer boundaries around her availability, not only with her daughter-in-law, but also with others and with demanding parts of herself–to prioritize her time and identify when she herself needed to be a "no show."

GUIDED IMAGERY FOR INVITING WAKING DREAMS

Facilitating a weekly guided imagery class for many years has repeatedly confirmed my trust in the efficacy of "healing dreams" that arise from guided imagery. Guided imagery research from several sources also confirms that guided sessions can bring highly targeted imagery and energy for working with the "dreamer's" primary concerns.[7]

An outline of the basics for seeking a healing dream is in Chapter 8. You will find the entire script, *Guided Imagery for Inviting a Healing Waking Dream*, at the end of the book and can record it for yourself, or you can download it from our website. Or you can just play background meditative music and guide yourself through the process. Set aside at least thirty minutes of uninterrupted time for meditative dreaming. Hold the intention that you will invite a meditative dream experience that will expand your understanding of who you are and the conflicts you feel. Below is a very short version of the script.

SCRIPT III: GUIDED IMAGERY FOR INVITING
A HEALING WAKING DREAM

Beginning to breathe and relax into a deep, centered, meditative space . . . progressively relaxing each part of your body . . . renewing . . . releasing . . . relaxing . . .

Noticing where you are holding tension . . . sending the warm energy of the breath to soothe and soften anyplace that needs to relax . . . sinking deeper and deeper into a centered place within . . .

Using all your senses . . . now imagining one of your inner sanctuary abodes . . . inviting Supportive Presence . . . allowing an image of a loving companion or companions to be with you . . .

Now, inviting a "waking dream," an experience from the realm of imagination intended to bring imagery that will help you further your healing and growth . . .

Suspending judgment . . . being fully present to whatever comes . . . entering into dialogue with a symbol from the dream if that feels appropriate . . . including your Supportive Presence in the dialogue if you like . . .

Concluding your interaction when you feel you have at least one clear experience to bring back . . . and whether you understand the waking dream or not, expressing gratitude for the power of the imagination and for the presence of support . . .

Making a mental note of what you want to bring back from the waking dream . . .

Knowing that you can return to your waking dream whenever you choose, slowly begin to return to ordinary waking consciousness . . . knowing that every time you set aside time to go inward to a centered place . . . you nourish your body . . . you nourish your mind . . . you nourish your spirit.

If at any point during the guided imagery experience you feel threatened or frightened, bring your attention back to your breath and to your progressive relaxation. Continue a guided imagery waking dream only when you feel fully supported and safe.

After returning to ordinary waking consciousness:

- Take time to record your experience. Write your reflections in your journal. Pay particular attention to how you are responding in the waking dream.

- Later explore symbols from your waking dream with basic Symbol Appreciation questions.

- Share your experience with a supportive friend, therapist, dream circle, or guided imagery group if you have the opportunity.

- Continue to re-enter this waking dream and allow it to develop. Or, keep seeking a new healing waking dream until you reach a felt-experience of new relationship with before-unexplored aspects of your life.

UGLY DOG AND SLUDGE

One night when her husband was away for the third time in a month and Amy felt particularly depressed, she decided to seek support through guided imagery. After putting on background music and breathing into a relaxed and centered place, Amy entered an inner sanctuary and invited Supportive Presence. A compassionate ally Amy calls Sophia appeared. Amy then asked for a waking dream that would help clarify and transform her depression.

Waking Dream: Ugly Dog

I am in a protected space behind a sand dune, warm
and sheltered from the wind. I can hear the rhythm of
the surf and the distant cries of sea gulls. I settle into a
sense of peace, yet I still feel very sad. I open my heart to
ask for an experience that will lift my depression. I wait.

177

Sensing something beside me, I look down and see a small, ugly black dog beside my feet. I jerk away because I recognize the dog as one who scared me badly when I was about seven. The dog is staring up at me. I feel threatened but remember that I have invited an experience that will help me. I take a deep breath and ask the dog, "What have you come to teach me"?

Our dialogue is a mixture of actual conversation and the mingling of thoughts that seem to belong to both Ugly Dog and me. It is very strange, but feels very real. The gist of what I take away is this:

---- Ugly Dog is powerful instinctual energy that once scared me and now can help me.

---- Ugly Dog was abandoned, starved, and angry. In my own way, I am abandoned, starved, and angry. I need to claim and honor these parts of myself. I need to let these parts of me know I love them and will integrate them into my life.

---- Ugly Dog was independent, resourceful, persistent, aggressive, and totally self-reliant. I can become more independent, resourceful, persistent, aggressive, and self-reliant in my relationship with my husband and with everyone else in my life.

---- Ugly Dog became fiercely loyal to my uncle, who gave him a chance for new life. I now have a chance for new life. I have new tools for tapping into my inner resources. I can be loyal in developing this new life.

Amy continued to ponder her meeting with Ugly Dog. His image stirred a sense of increasing compassion, and her insights from the dream fueled a sense of resolve. Nevertheless, Amy's depression returned each time her husband left town. After discussing her concern with the Dream Circle, Amy decided to use guided imagery to ask the depression itself to become an image with whom she could communicate. From her sanctuary and with Ugly Dog at her side, Amy asked the depression to take on size, shape, personality—to become a living image and to talk to her. Slowly, a large, slimy lump of coal appeared. It had short stubby legs and long slimy arms.

When Amy asked the Six Magic Questions, the slimy lump mumbled through a long thin crack that served as its mouth: "My name is Sludge. My purpose is to feed the heat. What I like about me is that I'm good fuel. What I hate is that no one wants to touch me. What I desire the most is to become a dancing flame. What I most fear is that no one will recognize my worth."

When Amy asked, "What do you want to teach me?" Sludge replied, "I want you to find the fire that is uniquely yours."

Amy was able to feel compassion and direct it toward the lump of coal. She imagined the energy of light surrounding and penetrating this strange unattractive being. The light became an intense laser beam. Gradually, the slimy lump of coal transformed into a small, perfect diamond. Amy has re-entered this experience many times, and each time has felt a shift in her depression. She also imagines holding the diamond and feeling its warmth when she senses the darkness of depression approaching.

YOUR OWN REFLECTIONS

1. Be on the lookout for encounters with synchronicity. Write down the longings and questions for which your soul is seeking answers. Be ready to notice experiences of meaningful coincidences in waking situations that speak to you in a special way.

2. Today explore an emotionally charged waking event with dream appreciation techniques. Describe the event. Look at key elements as metaphors. Ask questions as if the waking event holds clues for clarifying and enriching your responses to life.

3. Today pay particular attention to what surprises you. Explore your surprises for symbolic meaning.

4. Enter a relaxed state of deep meditation and invite a guided imagery dream that can help expand your life and bring healing energy. Release expectation. Suspend judgment. Allow an experience to develop. Explore the experience in the same way you explore a dream from sleep. Keep in mind that all dreams come in the service of health and wholeness.

5. Keep asking yourself: Which of my attitudes, perceptions, beliefs, ways of thinking, or patterns of behavior limit my abilities to make creative responses. How can I heal and grow from the "dreams" I encounter both when asleep and when awake?

6. If you are a caregiver or health professional, you may want to offer to read to the dreamer the script for seeking a healing waking dream. You can be a supportive companion while your dreamer explores the experience.

10

Honoring and Integrating Healing Imagery

Throughout this book, we have talked about "honoring" and integrating the energies of healing dreams and "waking" dreams. We honor the gifts when we rekindle the imagery and engage it with respect and appreciation. Through this process we become conscious of the healing energy the imagery holds. There are many ways to rekindle the imagery.

Honoring begins when you record your dreams. The process continues as you explore the images and energies through meditation, journaling, expressive arts, or expressive movement. You also can create "dream tasks," and you can share your dreams in a dream circle or with caring others. Any form of dream work honors the dream when it is done with an attitude of appreciation and with the intention to bring the energies into waking life.

GATHERING YOUR SYMBOLS

It is helpful to keep track of your personal healing symbols. Worksheet #3, *My Healing Imagery*, in the back of this book provides a place for you to begin to keep your list. Healing symbols are unique to each person; many evolve over time, changing form as the emotional and spiritual energies shift. For example, in Margaret's dreams, the nightmare imagery of Rotting Bird and Black Snake transformed into hope-inspired images of Golden Bird and Rainbow Snake.

Golden Bird has been Margaret's guide into long awaited spiritual experiences since it first appeared. Most dreamers have powerful symbols that carry healing energy through the years, but they also gather continually emerging new imagery.

Some of your most powerful symbols may be your images of inner sanctuary and Supportive Presence that come through guided imagery journeys. When Sam invites Supportive Presence into his meditations, the image of Job, the Leper-now-turned Inner Healer appears. Smokey the Bear often shows up for Jay. Although Golden Bird is a constant companion, Margaret has been surprised to find that occasionally, the presence of the Virgin Mary comes to be with her. When Margaret was a little girl, she went twice with a friend to a nearby Catholic Church. The colorful windows and life-like statues stirred her imagination and deep longings. Recently Mother Mary has appeared in Margaret's self-guided imagery meditations, and the encounters have felt very sensate and powerful.

PAINT, QUILT, WRITE

Drawing, painting, working with clay, creating mandalas or collages—indeed, expressing any form of art—can be a way to keep healing energy alive and growing. Most integrative wellness centers offer classes not only in the visual arts but also in writing and journaling. Some have knitting and quilting groups where the focus is on "stitching" as a meditative practice. Recent research studies cited in anthologies of integrative oncology confirm that engaging in any of the expressive arts impacts both quality of life and the immune system in positive ways.[1] Most members of dream circles in cancer centers participate in expressive arts classes. They bring poems and art pieces based on their dreams to share with the dream circle.

Margaret brings quilting material to every circle meeting. She feels quilting is a metaphor for how she participates in her own healing process. Last week, after sharing a dream about her conflicting emotions, Margaret held up a piece of her work and said, "Four more squares and my quilt will be ready to put together. My quilt will be a collage of the pieces of who I am. I feel I'm quilting the fragments of my wholeness as a personal and unique design."

Jay draws many of his dreams as cartoons. For a long time he was reluctant to share his drawings with the group. Overcoming his reluctance to claim his talent has been a big step in Jay's healing process. Several weeks ago Jay shared a dream about his job. He displayed a series of caricatures of his boss, and everyone laughed. Jay commented, "The dreams seem more vivid when I draw. They come alive, and I can really interact with them. Sometimes the dream story just keeps on going as I sketch, and I can better sense the meaning. Drawing my dreams also helps me to remember them."

Begin to play with your own dreams through expressive arts. You may want to:

- Create a special dream journal. Adorn the cover with your personal symbols, or set aside a place inside the journal to sketch them.

- Create a small altar on which you place symbols that you are given, find, or make. Light a candle in the center whenever you are doing meditative work.

- Create a mandala as you meditate with your dream. Draw a circle and then create your artwork within the circle. Meditate, using your mandala as the focus.

- Rewrite your dream, adding a missing beginning or ending, or rewrite it from the point of view of one of the other characters. As you write, maintain a meditative state.

- Rewrite the dream as a fairy tale, poem, or prayer.

- Underline the metaphors when you record your dreams. Rewrite inspiring metaphors as affirmations that you can post on your mirror or refrigerator. For example: Emily has posted on her bathroom mirror "Stay Balanced," "Relax," "I put my baggage down," "My strength returns." These were phrases from her recorded dreams.

- If you play a musical instrument, close your eyes and feel the emotions of your dream as you play. This is a powerful way to "embody" the dream.

WALK, DANCE, SWIM

As you walk, dance, swim, or move in any way, you can intentionally savor your imagery while you move. You can imagine energy moving into every cell. Many cancer wellness centers offer yoga, tai chi, qigong and fitness programs facilitated by professionals trained to work with people in treatment or recovery. Recent studies of benefits of the above-mentioned practices are enumerated in integrative oncology anthologies.[2] When the positive benefits associated with healing imagery are added to meditative movement, the positive effects of both movement and imagery are compounded, as Rachel reported in her journal:

> Today I went to yoga again, and for the first time
> after all these weeks, I could feel energy in each part
> of my body as we did the body scan. So I invited my
> dream of finding gas for my car, and I imagined the
> gasoline as a special healing fuel that I could send
> to each part of my body. With each yoga pose, I
> imagined the fuel flowing freely to the places in my
> body that needed it most. These were new sensations.
> I actually felt energy in specific places in my body!

Any form of movement can become a meditative activity.

- You may want to focus on one of your healing experiences the next time you take a walk. Imagine the energy of the imagery moving with each step you take.

- You may want to focus on a healing image in yoga or tai chi class. In time you will develop increased sensitivity and the ability to perceive and influence the presence of energy in each part of your body.

- You can enter into an image, feel and move. In a meditative state, you can be the cat, the tree, the snake. When you are the image, you can express yourself through purposeful movement.

DREAM TASKS

With the intention to bring energy of imagery into waking life, you can create small, concrete, doable tasks for acting upon the gifts of the dream. Please review Sam's dream and the symbol association process in Chapter 2.

- Choose a symbol from your dream that feels compelling to you. List your associations. (Sam chose the Kayak as his symbol.)

- Circle associations that might help you in your waking life situation. (Sam circled a sense of balance, a sense of exhilaration, a sense of adventure. He selected these energies as ones that might help in his current crisis.)

- Create a simple activity, a concrete action that you can manifest in a timely fashion to bring these energies into a waking experience. (Sam called a friend and planned a short hike for the next weekend to honor a sense of adventure.)

- You may also, or instead, create a small symbolic gesture. (Sam might have found a poster of a kayak and put it on his wall.) The important thing is to make a conscious connection between your symbolic act and the dream.

- If the dream comments on your body, you can create an activity to honor the comment. In Rachel's dream, she was driving her car at high speed. To honor the dream's invitation to slow down, Rachel stayed home from work for a day to rest and read.

- You also can create relationship tasks. First make a list of energies you need for relating to yourself and others in a more authentic and creative way. Let your dreams be a guide. Attitudes and behaviors that need to be considered are often displayed by the shadow figures in your dreams. Please review Chapter 5.

- Keep a list of the character traits of your shadow figures. Ask yourself where a characteristic would be helpful if you could express it in a balanced way. Set the goal to express this characteristic in a small, balanced way the next time you are in a situation that calls for a more creative response.

- If the dream is trying to help you enlarge a present pattern of thought, or to expand a present belief or attitude, then participate in a situation with the intention to enlarge your present view. After her *Tarnished and Abandoned* dream, Emily went to a lecture on the topic "How to Support Your Partner."

- If a dream offers a new perspective on a past or present situation, do something as a gesture to respond in a new way. After her "Edna" dream, Amy bought another large canvas, to paint her anger and grief once again. She vowed she would show it to her husband and mother and talk to them about what her new painting style means to her.

- If the dream is trying to bring you into deeper relationship with your spiritual life, create a simple, concrete response. After her "Golden Bird" dream, Margaret began a practice of daily journaling in which she prefaced each morning's entry with: *Thank you for imagery and energy that offer a way into larger life. Please keep me open to Supportive Presence throughout the day.*

DAILY PRACTICE

Meditating and journaling on a regular basis can help you to bring energy of healing imagery into the body and to integrate the energy into waking life. Try to set aside special time to meditate each day. Begin with progressive relaxation. You can read Script I at the end of the book or listen to the recording from our website. When you are in a deeply centered, meditative space, focus your full attention on one of your healing images. Savor the energy.

Each night before you go to sleep, review your day and reflect on when and where you felt a sense of connection. Notice when and where you felt separate and alone. Where did you feel surprise? Reflect on when and where you felt off balance and out of sync. Consciously ask for guidance through your dreams. Each morning, record your dreams and write reflections in your dream journal. Get into a rhythm of round-the-clock dialogue with the symbolic realm.

Emily is developing a daily practice. Each night she journals about her concerns from the day. Each morning she records her dreams and looks for connections.

Today I tried to call Andrew. We haven't talked in almost a week, but he didn't return my call. I'm asking my dreams to bring energy to help me move through the next few days.

Old Rope Swing

In this dream, I'm a little girl swinging on the old rope swing at my grandmother's. Soaring up, soaring back. I feel exhilaration! I will try to stop and re-enter this sense of exhilaration throughout the day, especially when I slip into my Andrew depression and anxieties. I'll re-imagine the positive sensations as a way to keep my emotions in balance.

- Each day, focus on one of your healing images. Like Emily, re-enter a positive sensation. Breathe it in. Savor it in your body, mind, and soul. Take it in as your daily "dream medicine."

- Each day, be on the alert for experiences in waking life that trigger strong emotion and surprise. Let them speak to you as if they are dreams.

MOVING LIGHT IN

When you have clearly identified your healing symbols, you can direct their energy through self-guided imagery journeys to targeted areas of concern. You can direct energy of a personal symbol to specific areas of the body or to specific emotional and spiritual conflicts. You will find Script IV, "Guided Imagery for Integrating Healing Symbols" at the end of the book. You may download it from our website.

IMAGERY FOR THE BODY

- First, bring one of your healing images into a deep meditative place and savor the symbol with all your senses.

- Allow the image to become so vivid that it begins to seem realer than real. If the symbol begins to change, allow change to happen. Trust deep wisdom to shape the image as needed for any given situation. For example, one time the Inner Healer appeared to Sam as an ordinary person; the next time, he seemed to be a disembodied spirit. Allow the image that finally settles into your meditative space to impact your mind, body, and spirit. Breathe in the energy.

- Imagine that your chosen image slowly transforms into a concentrated form of palpable energy, perhaps as a stream of light, perhaps with color, heat, or vibration. Imagine breathing in the light, taking it inside your body. Imagine the light as multiple streams of life energy moving freely from your head to your toes and from your toes to your head. Imagine energy flowing freely, light moving unimpeded to surround and penetrate every organ, every tissue, and every cell. Allow the energy to saturate every cell in your body, freeing every aspect of the body to function in the way that is needed for optimum healing and growth.

- If you want to focus the energy into a particular place in your body, you may place your hands on a spot that needs special tending. With your imagination, focus the energy of your image as a powerful beam that both surrounds and penetrates the part of your body that needs special attention and care. Imagine warm and soothing energy moving through your hands, surrounding, penetrating, and doing whatever work is needed to bring about healing. You may want to imagine a tumor shrinking, a torn muscle knitting, white blood cells multiplying. Imagine whatever needs to happen to be happening.

- In your imagination, move back and forth between focusing on a specific area of the body and on focusing into the healing image you first brought to the meditation. Feel your special image generating the energy that you now focus into your body. Imagine transformation within your body. As you breathe in and out, rest in the sensation of wholeness.

- Finally, feeling restored and renewed, rest in a sense of stillness and balance. Express gratitude. Slowly return to waking consciousness when you are ready.

You do not have to imagine changes in the body in a physiologically correct way. Belleruth Naparstek reminds us that "several practitioners in the field—Jeanne Achterberg and Michael Samuels among them—hypothesize that metaphoric imagery is even more powerful than the rigidly 'anatomically correct' sort. They theorize that the right brain is just naturally more predisposed toward symbols (you can look at the content of your dreams and see how true this is). Moreover, psychology has long felt that the indirectness of metaphors, which don't come at us head-on, can cut through the resistance to change that we might have." [3]

IMAGERY FOR PAIN

Before Amy's mastectomy, Laura helped her create a guided imagery CD to soothe the pain from surgery. Amy selected imagery from her dream in which she was filled with empowering energy as she rubbed her hands over beautiful, highly polished stone sculpture. After breathing and relaxing into a deep meditative space, Amy re-entered the dream experience. Then she imagined the vibrant, warm energy from the stone coming through her hands and flowing freely through her body. Next, she placed her hands on her chest and imagined focusing the energy into and around the area of her breast surgery. She imagined the energy surrounding and penetrating the area. Amy used her CD in conjunction with prescribed pain medication. She was able to discontinue the medication sooner than the doctor predicted. Many studies confirm the efficacy of using imagery for the alleviation of pain. Summaries of these studies are available in anthologies of integrative oncology.[4]

IMAGERY FOR TREATMENT SESSIONS

Doctors' appointments and treatment sessions are stressful no matter what illness you have, and as studies have shown for many years, using relaxation skills during these times helps to alleviate the stress. When healing imagery is added to relaxation, the benefits are compounded. Using relaxation plus imagery allows the body's healing systems to get maximum benefit from medical treatment. Research studies show the benefits of using imagery both before and after surgery.[5] In recent years, guided imagery CDs related to preparing for and healing from surgery sometimes have been paid for by insurance.[6]

In some treatment settings, cancer patients are offered guided imagery CDs to use during chemotherapy and radiation treatments. In the IASD Cancer Project, a few dream circle members have recorded personal CDs with their own healing dream imagery to use in conjunction with their conventional medical treatment. Amy's journal reveals how helpful her personal CD was before going for a CT scan:

Today I'm going for my first scan since the mastectomy. I know how important it is to stay centered and calm. My personal CD helped me center and soothe pain after my surgery. Today I'll try to re-enter my sculpture dream and again feel the warm energy from the smooth stones that before so filled me with a sense of healing. I'll listen to the CD before I go for my scan and stay grounded in the energy so that I can stay calm.

IMAGERY FOR THE MIND

We have talked previously about dialoguing with emotional or mental issues and conflicts. Images of your concerns, your pain, your symptoms, or your resistance can personify and become images that can teach you about parts of yourself and issues that need your loving attention. Please review the section labeled "Personification" in Chapter 6.

We emphasize in this chapter the importance of embodying the new image that has transformed from the old image. It is the transformed imagery that carries the energy of healing.

- After your image of concern has become a new image, if this image feels healing, allow it to become a form of palpable energy, perhaps multiple streams of light, perhaps with color or heat, or vibration. Imagine the streams of this energy now coursing through your body; energy flowing freely; streams of energy moving unimpeded, clearing away any clutter in your mind, sweeping it clean, filling your heart with light, bringing a sense of spacious stillness, peace, and calm.

- With each breath, imagine moving down, down, down into this centered place of stillness. Savor the silence. Savor your sense of peace and calm.

- Allow your emotions to settle into a pleasing configuration—perhaps like colors of a kaleidoscope settling into a beautiful design. Rest in the beauty. Rest in the presence of healing energy.

RELEASING THE LION

To further your work with inner conflict, you may want to concretize your meditative journeys by creating small rituals of letting go.[7] Name the thought pattern, the attitude, the belief, or the behavior pattern that keeps you stuck and that keeps repeating in your life and in your dreams. For example, like Jay, you may feel that it is hard to speak up for yourself or, like Sam, that you are holding on to resentment. Whatever you name—guilt, shame, negligence, selfishness—whatever you would like to transform or leave behind, make or find an image that symbolizes it. Next, perform a concrete, symbolic act such as burning the symbol, setting it adrift, dropping it over a cliff, tying it to your wrist and then cutting the cord, anything that symbolizes letting it go. For example, Margaret has become aware of her incessant need for control. She made a little lion out of clay as a symbol of her need for control. Then, with clear intention to release this need, she took the unfired lion outdoors and set him in her garden where she could watch as he weathered away in the rain.

IMAGERY FOR THE SPIRIT

If you are longing for deep connection with spiritual life, you can look to your list of healing images and also to your images of Supportive Presence. Gather them up and take them into your heart. Allow the energies of your images to stir your emotions with palpable energy. Focus on your yearning for spiritual connection, your longing for a sense of relationship with power and support greater than yourself. Permit your healing images to become energy that will take you across a bridge into a realm of great mystery and spirit.

Breathe deeply and imagine the energy flowing as streams throughout your body. Perhaps you may imagine the energy as light, perhaps accompanied by color, heat or cool, or vibration. Allow your soul to be filled. Allow your whole being to shift into balance as the energy flows. Sink into a sense of connection, rest, and peace. Breathe in the energy of gratitude. Breathe out the energy of blessing.

BIRD, SNAKE, MOTHER MARY

Each day, Margaret takes time to meditate with imagery from her dreams. First she sends healing energy of Golden Bird or Rainbow Snake to her pelvic region, the area of the ovarian cancer. She imagines the energy as golden light, penetrating and dissolving the tumors. She imagines every cell in her body opening to healing light. She breathes in the energy of renewal to nourish and strengthen healthy cells.

Margaret then focuses on her longing for spiritual connection. Then she invites an image of compassion to be with her. She reports to the group that most of the time she simply follows the energy of Bird or Snake into a place of stillness.

As mentioned earlier, Margaret has occasional encounters with Mother Mary. In dream circles across the country, Margaret is one among many cancer survivors who speak of finding renewed spiritual connection through dream and guided imagery encounters with compassionate feminine presence. This feminine image may take on many guises, but when she appears, she brings a sense of comfort and blessing. We find that many who participate in cancer dream circles or guided imagery groups discover a new relationship with the spiritual realm, a relationship grounded in sensate, personal experience. They also report that these personal encounters in no way conflict with their "religious" views. Instead, many report that their personal experiences with inspiring symbols actually help to deepen their relationship with a lost or forgotten religious heritage.[8]

MOVING LIGHT OUTWARD

An important part of any meditative practice is to deepen a sense of connection, not only to all the parts of oneself, but to others, and to all aspects of the world and beyond. With guided imagery, you can send healing energy to other people and to situations in the world and beyond.

- Bring a healing image into your heart. Savor it with all your senses.

- Allow the image to become the energy of light. Breathe it into your heart. Allow your sense of compassion and blessing to expand with each breath. Allow compassion to fill every cell in your body.

- Now, imagine directing the light outward toward specific others that you know, allowing the light to surround and penetrate them as you hold each person clearly in your imagination.

- Imagine directing the light outward toward unknown others, toward the world, the planet, and beyond.

One of the most researched areas in integrative medicine is guided mindfulness and compassion meditation. The positive effects of developing compassion are affirmed by a preponderance of evidence-based studies.[9]

CULTIVATING SUPPORTIVE ATTITUDES.

In support of healing and growth, dreams ask the dreamer to cultivate attitudes and behaviors that lead to inner transformation and larger life. Dreams ask you to cultivate attitudes and responses that facilitate relationship with the symbolic realm. Building a relationship with the realm of the dream takes a tremendous amount of courage and persistent determination. After all, dream wisdom is usually in conflict with the ego's agenda. The ego likes to feel safe and comfortable. Dreams invite and often demand that the dreamer give up safety and comfort and venture into risky places of the unknown. The ego loves the familiar and hates change. The ego wants disturbing situations and people to just go away or be changed so that life can be the same once more. But dreams focus on and often demand that the ego allow or even promote the death of old ego patterns. Death of habitual patterns frees the deeper personality to move toward healing and wholeness. Sam often reflects on how he can nurture supportive attitudes, both in himself and in others, as he does in this journal entry:

> My dreams are asking me to face up to my inner leper, my inner cripple, my inner healer, my inner lover. It's hard to face up to most of the parts of myself that show up in my dreams. What attitudes and behaviors do I need to cultivate so that I can more readily accept the parts of myself that are all out of balance? Often in the Dream Circle, we talk about helpful attitudes.
>
> Compassion is the key—first toward myself, and then others. Courage, patience, longing for a sense of meaning and connection—I try to nurture these. A sense of awe, a sense of gratitude, an open heart and expanding mind—I try to nurture these too. Dreams speak in symbols and metaphors, so I try to nurture the questions "What in my life is or was like this? Where did I or do I interact in this way?"

A sense of humor and the ability to play—these qualities are essential, but very hard for a serious guy like me. The hardest one is a willingness to release old patterns that no longer contribute to my healing and growth. I also forget to welcome surprise. More and more I'm trying to hold lightly the tension of paradox—to look at both sides of my conflicts and trust that a new synthesis will come. Compassion, courage, and patience—these are the three attitudes that I hope for the most.

YOUR OWN REFLECTIONS

1. The *My Healing Imagery* worksheet in the back of the book provides a place to list your healing symbols. Include your **Healing Sanctuaries** and your images of **Supportive Presence**, as well as **Peaceful Settings**, **Surprises** that help you change direction, **Situations of Renewal and Hope**, Images that bring a **Sense of Guidance**, **Numinous Imagery**, and **Imagery Transformed from Nightmares**. Visit your lists often.

2. Explore your dreams through expressive art, music, or meditative movements. Do you find your insights and energy expanding?

3. Today, create a dream task from one of your recent dreams. Let it be playful and fun.

4. Begin to develop your own personal practices for embodying and integrating your healing imagery. Express gratitude for the mystery of dreams and for the power of the imagination to bring healing imagery into your life.

5. If you are a caregiver or health professional, you can brainstorm with your dreamer to help choose a meaningful way to integrate and express the energies in waking life.

11
CONTINUING THE JOURNEY

Laura has called the dream circle members to come in for a special session. She is preparing for an interview with the editor of an integrative health magazine who asked her to write an article about dream work with cancer patients. Laura will record the meeting and get permission to use the dreams and comments. All the dream circle members have been able to come.

When Margaret enters the room, she announces she just got a call that her blood-work results show her CA 125 is suddenly very high. Her doctor wants her to come in for a CAT scan.[1] She is worried that this might mean she is no longer in remission. As Margaret is speaking, the group becomes still. Her announcement has a numbing effect on everyone in the room.

Laura gently invites everyone into a guided progressive relaxation. When the group has breathed and relaxed into a deep, still, centered place, Laura invokes imagery and energy for connection and hope. Breathing in, breathing out, the group settles into supportive space of peaceful connection. After allowing several minutes for savoring the energy, Laura invites everyone to return slowly to ordinary consciousness.

"I remind you that you can remain connected and centered even as we begin to talk about how working with dreams can help you move through the cancer experience. I'd like each of you to say whatever you want to say without interruption; but also, I hope we can dialogue together with several questions. As I said in my email request, I will record this session today. I'll send each of you a copy of the article before I submit it. If there is anything you want to change or don't want me to include, I'll comply."

Margaret asks to speak first. "I have to say that I'm reacting to today's unwanted news in a less panicked way compared to the way I reacted to the news that led to my first diagnosis. I'm very anxious about my elevated CA 125, but in the guided relaxation, as we went into a deep, meditative space, I felt myself responding to supportive energy within and all around me. My initial reaction of fear began transform. As I relaxed, I slipped back into a dream I had last night. It's title is 'Solid Ground.'

> "In the dream, I'm crossing what seems like miles of muddy fields. In the dream, it's raining at first; then slowly streaks of daylight begin to break through the dark. I'm taking one tentative step after another. Each time I hope I won't sink into the mud. And I don't. I seem to have an intuitive feel for the firm spots. As the light gets stronger, I become bolder, and like a kindergarten child playing hopscotch, I move quickly from solid spot to solid spot. I finally reach a place that's like a small oasis. I sink down on the soft grass to rest. From this angle on the ground, I can see that I have crossed a huge expanse that looks like a muddy lake. In the dream, I feel relief and gratitude."

The group is listening with focused attention. Margaret continues, "This morning when I woke up, I wrote the dream in my journal and I then I wrote down these affirmations. Every morning I do this with my dreams. I call the affirmations my little dream gifts. Throughout the day I re-imagine the gifts and repeat the affirmations." Margaret reads from her journal:

Dawn breaks from the dark rain.

I am bold and playful like a kindergarten child.

I am resting on solid ground.

An oasis of relief enfolds me.

Gratitude.

"The call from my oncologist's office this morning was a shock. I was frightened, and I still am. But the experience of last night's dream helped prepare me for today. The energy of the dream made an impact. The dream gifts I record each day in my journal are reliable resources. I trust my new tools for navigating this journey through cancer and through life. I trust imagery and energies that are always speaking."

Laura responds quietly. "Thank you so much, Margaret. Can you say a little more about the relationship you feel between your meditative dream practice and your outer life?"

Margaret takes a minute to reflect. "My dream-work practice helps me relate to the situations of my life as challenges and opportunities. Whether it's a 'waking' dream or a sleeping dream, when I seek out the symbols and metaphors, I find insights and energy for living more fully."

Margaret looks around the circle and gestures for someone else to speak.

Jay begins. "I think the biggest lesson I've learned from my dream work practice is that I was asking the wrong questions. I was asking *Why is this happening?* and *Why me? How can I get rid of this?* With new tools from the dream circle and all the classes here at the cancer center, I've learned to ask *What is this trying to show me, or to teach me? How can this help me to live in a better way?*

"When I was first diagnosed, I felt I had lost all control over my life. I also had scary dreams about being put down by my boss and former bosses and mean teachers from way back. Over time, I've built a relationship with my "inner critic." With active imagination, I've talked with the mean teacher and critical boss part of me. I've found him to be a very insecure guy. I also have built a relationship with my "inner victim." Turns out he's a part of me who finds it much easier to blame circumstances and other people than to take responsibility. As I get to know the different shadow parts of myself, and as they get to know each other, I find I have more clarity and options for making choices about my life."[2]

Jay pauses. "I can't think of anything else to say right now."

Amy waves her hand, and Laura nods in her direction. Amy addresses Jay. "When you spoke of new ways to respond to your life, I saw an image of a kaleidoscope. For me, dreams are like kaleidoscopes in that they take all the fragmented emotions and pieces and allow them to fall into ever-changing designs. I don't recall any dream that has told me precisely what to do. I don't recall any dream that has told me precisely how to fix things. Instead, like a kaleidoscope, my dreams present new artful designs saturated with light and color. These stir up my appreciation and hope. Jay, you mentioned loss of control. When I hold and turn a kaleidoscope in my hand, I feel I've gained a different kind of control. I feel drawn into the moment to be totally present to whatever is there."

Amy pauses and looks around the circle. "Last night I had a vivid dream. Then on top of it, I had a half-waking experience that has put me in touch with big insights and lots of energy. This feels very important."

Laura replies, "I see you brought your journal. Would you please read?"

Amy says, "I call this dream 'Waiting.'

> "I am waiting. I'm sitting in a corner of a dark room, but I can see into the room through two open doorways. I have multiple perspectives. My corner is like home plate of a baseball diamond. One doorway is between first and second base and the other is

between second and third base. Tables are set for a
big celebration; people are arriving, all engaged in
lively conversation. I'm waiting for an invitation to
join them. A handsome man moves from person to
person, greeting them as a gracious host. He doesn't
see me. I think maybe he will see me if I move. So
while I'm still sitting in my chair, I lean to the left;
then I lean to the right. Does he see me? I am not
seen. I continue to wait. I feel left out. I want to be
included. I wait."

Amy looks around at the members of the circle and says, "Then
I begin to wake up. I tell myself to stay in the dream. I'm aware that
I'm in a liminal state of consciousness between being asleep and
being awake. I've heard that this is a very creative state.[3] I tell myself
to move back into the dream. I tell myself to get up out of my corner,
to walk into the party. At this point, the dream changes. I call this
part 'Walking In.'

"Gathering up courage, I stand up and begin to walk
forward. I am aware of the two doorways, and it is as
if I'm somehow moving into the room through both
the doors at the same time. The man sees me and
smiles. We walk towards each other and embrace.
Then together we move from person to person,
embracing each guest. Now, I notice that beyond the
tables are large windows. Outside, the sun is shining
and flowers are blooming. I wake up again, this time
feeling full, or should I say fulfilled?"

The group wants to jump in with "If it were my dream . . . ," but
Laura turns to Amy and asks her to reflect on the insights and gifts
she will want to bring into her waking life.

Amy responds, "I have a solid, sensate experience of embracing
a part of my inner masculine that is symbolized by the handsome,

gracious host. I embrace him and also a room full of interesting parts of myself that are symbolized by the other guests. All are enjoying an inner celebration. This experience is a gift! I feel so very grateful. Too often, I long for others, especially my husband and my mother, to validate who I am. The dream gives me a solid experience of trusting the energies that are always within me and are always available. I feel it's the gift of inner validation.

"My big insight is that having done this half-awake dream re-entry one time, I can do it again and again. Whenever I first start waking up, I can choose to stay in the dream. As the dream develops, I can develop attitudes and responses that are more life-serving and creative. I can stay in the dream so my new responses can unfold. I know this will be hard. Taking that first step out of the corner of the room was one of the hardest things I've ever done."

Amy continues to reflect. "I'd like to say a little more about moving through the two doorways at the same time." Amy closes her eyes to re-imagine the experience.

"As I move from my corner and through the doors into the room, I'm very aware of multiple perspectives. It feels very natural to see the whole room from both sides. In my body, I feel expansion, yet a sense of synthesis. Maybe it's a metaphoric experience of integrating and centering. Since one door is on the left and the other is on the right, maybe the imagery reflects the simultaneous functioning of the rational, thinking left brain and the intuitive, right brain. Whatever the elements of the dream's creation, it was a vivid experience of coming to the center of myself from opposite sides. I know I'll ever forget it!"

Laura allows several moments for Amy's words to sink in and settle. Then she thanks Amy and nods to Rachel, who is looking as if she wants to speak

Rachel says, "Three things stand out for me about how dreams fit into my stress-reduction attempts. The first is that I really appreciate the support of people in this group. Of course, I also find support in every group here at the cancer center. So the second thing that stands out about the dream circle is that when we're gathering dream stories with their imagery and metaphors, we're coming face to face with powerful energy. It's like the symbols are alive. Just from the last few minutes we've all been able to feel the energy of holding a kaleidoscope, embracing the handsome host, resting on solid ground. Anytime we revisit these experiences with guided imagery, we'll be taking in 'good medicine.' It's the same with any healing symbol. Symbols bring energy that can change us.

"The third thing that stands out for me—and every day I feel this more and more—is my growing certainty that something big is guiding me into the fullest life I can possibly live. I'll give you an example from the past few days. It's a dream and then a synchronistic experience that have changed my whole lackadaisical attitude toward diet and exercise. I call the dream 'Food on Fire.'

"In my dream I wander into an enormous banquet hall. Little round tables are set with fine china and linens. A rose graces the center of each table. An orchestra plays softly on a small stage. Long tables around the edges of the room are piled with every imaginable kind of food. I begin to serve my plate. I take a small filet, then a big baked potato with a decorative cheese design on top. Noticing a sumptuous dessert table, I refrain from putting anything else on my plate so that later, I'll have room for chocolate samples. I'm proud of myself for being so discriminating.

"I join three other women at one of the round tables. I recognize them from the cancer center. As I'm placing my plate on the table, it bursts into flames. I can feel heat on my hands and arms. I scream and drop the plate. Others scream. I wake up hating this dream."

Rachel continues, "Two days later I came here to the center for a nutrition class. What was it about? *Inflammation!* The entire talk was about foods that contribute to inflammatory reactions and about how inflammation contributes to tumor formation and growth.[4] All through the class I remembered my banquet plate flaming up. I felt the heat and my terrified reaction. I said to myself, 'Someone is looking after me. This dream is really speaking to me.'

"For the first time, I opened myself to advice being given in the class. For the first time, I made a commitment to read one of the nutrition books.[5] When I got home, I picked up the phone and registered for a recommended twelve-week exercise class."

The group sits in appreciative silence. Laura and everyone in the circle thank Rachel for sharing. Emily looks at Sam. He says quickly, "You go next."

Emily begins, "This has nothing to do with the article, but I want to update everyone on Andrew. Last week, he got a small promotion at work, and he feels good being the manager of a new project. He also registered at an on-line university and will start working on a master's degree. He's happier. When we've met for lunch a couple of times, I've felt very sure of how much I love him. I'm also more certain about his love for me. I'm not panicked anymore. I'm okay with waiting, and I'm no longer totally attached to the outcome.

"Which brings me to how I describe the relationship between my mind-body practices and my cancer journey—actually, my life journey, since cancer is just one piece of the puzzle of my life. Through the mind-body practices offered here at the center, I've come to trust the reality of an underlying, life-promoting process. It's the big something that Rachel just mentioned. It's the ever-flowing wellspring bubbling up from the deep that we imagine in guided imagery. Healing imagery comes to me in dreams, synchronistic experiences, and guided imagery. The energy grows and nourishes me as I meditate, journal, or express myself through art, music, or movement practices. Since our last dream circle, I had a dream that helps me say what I'm trying to say. The title is 'Disconnected from the Source.'

"In the dream, I'm in my kitchen enjoying a second cup of morning coffee. I'm thankful that I'm warm and protected from last night's ice storm. All of a sudden, the lights go out. The hum of the furnace stops. I jump up and head straight for the light switch. Nothing happens when I flip it, so I reach out to tighten the light bulb in a nearby lamp. No effect. I look out the window. Power lines crisscross the front yard. I wake up feeling frustrated.

"The day after the dream, I took some time to write in my journal." Margaret opens her journal and reads,

"I smile at the dream's metaphors for how my ego reacts to crisis. My ego is determined to fix this! Flip the switch, tighten the light bulb! My ego focuses on fixing the symptoms to bring the lights back on. But the real problem is my broken connection with the generator far away. My real problem is that I'm disconnected from the source. The broken lines strewn across the yard are a graphic symbol showing the real problem."

Emily looks around the circle. "How to fix the broken connection? How to reconnect? How to stay connected? For me, these are the real questions. If I had the answers, I think I would have the key to healing. I meditated with the dream. I went back into it. In the meditation, a Georgia Power truck pulled in my driveway and several workers in hard hats got out and began reconnecting the broken power lines. So I took out my journal and wrote this: 'Thank you for the image of workers with hard hats. Whenever I feel disconnected from the generator, may I reimagine the image and trust the mystery of becoming reconnected.'"

Emily shrugs. "Of course I need to reflect on who or what the hard hat workers symbolize. I imagine they're my dream work and guided imagery and all my meditative practices. But the mystery remains. And the symbol of the generator, the power station, and the power that flows out over the wires—this is the mystery at the center of the healing journey. I've said enough right now. It's time for Sam to talk."

Sam stretches in his chair and begins, "This, too, has nothing to do with the article, but you'll be happy to know I've just had two dates with a really special woman. Hey, don't look so surprised!"

"Who is she?" Amy asks with excitement.

"Where'd you meet her?" Jay asks at the same time.

Sam grins and says, "She's a new counselor in our clinic who joined us last month. She's been divorced two years. I'll keep you posted on how things go. I feel closer to you folks in this circle than to most anybody. Laura, you can say this in the article if you want to. In this group, as we share each other's dream stories and guided imagery journeys, we're all connected in the symbolic realm. And that's a very deep place of connection.

"So what is important for me to say about the relationship between my mind-body practices and my healing journey? Emily's dream speaks to me. It invites me to focus on connection to the generator, to the life source. The way I experience my own connection to the healing process is through dialogue with healing imagery—like with Job, who has become my Inner Healer. I kindle my healing images by re-imagining them. Then I send the energy into my body. I did this as a daily practice throughout the radiation treatments. Most days I call on my imagery intentionally to touch into sensate feelings of supportive presence. Then I access and direct the energy inward to places in my body and mind, and outward to others. I also allow imagery to take me into new emotional and spiritual places. For me, any of my healing images serves as a match to ignite energy.

"Changing subjects, I think it's important to point out the paradoxical nature of the healing journey. Dreams and imagery that mark the way of transformation keep me mindful of the unity of light and dark, of health and disease, of life and death. Through dreams and guided imagery I personally experience destruction and chaos as well as creation and peace. Symbols of death and rebirth are intricately intertwined. I try to ask of every dream experience, 'What needs to die? What is trying to come to life?' I also keep reminding myself that the healing process is bringing me into a state of wholeness, not a state of perfection.

"I brought a short recent dream that illustrates for me what I'm trying to say." Sam turns to his journal. "This one is called 'Running Into the Crossfire.'

> "I'm back on the street where I grew up. It's dark, but I can see that the neighborhood is very run down. It feels dangerous. As I approach my old house, I see it is surrounded by policemen with their guns drawn. One yells at me to move back. This is a drug raid. I know that my young cousin is inside. I have ignored rumors he is a drug dealer. I dash toward the house to warn him. Maybe I can help him escape. Shots ring out from both sides. I'm hit. Slammed from two sides. I see blood on my jacket. As I'm falling, the light grows bright. Waking up, I know that I'm someplace I've never been before. In the dream, I feel very much at peace.

"This dream has totally shaken me. It's one of those numinous dreams that rattle my soul. Every time I re-enter it, my heart pounds, I can hardly breathe, and I get all sweaty. It's one of the few times I remember actually dying in a dream. It's my only experience of deliberately running into crossfire. I know I'm looking at big time transformation because I feel the huge impact in my body. So, just as

I've talked in the past with my Inner Healer with active imagination, I've been talking with my inner drug dealer and my inner policeman. I've learned a lot about these parts of myself.

"The inner drug dealer has taught me about the part of me who tries to deny feelings and to be numbed out. He came into my life way back when I was a young teenager and my dad left. Since having the dream, I've been trying to juggle the energies of the drug dealer in a more balanced way. I was really numbed out when I was going through my divorce, and this helped get me through. But now I need to encourage this part of myself to risk feeling the feelings whatever they are. I need to develop objectivity and the ability to achieve distance and separateness without numbing out.

"The inner policeman is the part of me who constantly warns about following the rules. But this part of me too often judges others and stymies instinctual and creative parts of me. He puts these parts of me in jail. Since the dream, I'm trying to help him balance the ways he tries to keep law and order. I also want to make sure his efforts don't kill somebody, including parts of me."

Sam turns to Laura and says, "That's enough from me. You said you have some questions for us to discuss?"

"Thank you, Sam. Thank you all for bringing in dreams and comments. All of you model so well what the dream-work process with guided imagery is all about. All of you help articulate the healing nature of the work. I'd like to ask you now to help put together a list of themes you have discovered to be integral to the healing journey. Please talk about some of your dream themes."

THE HEALING JOURNEY

Margaret speaks quickly. "The first theme I think of is 'wakeup call.' Like Rotting Bird and Black Snake, all my nightmares seem to be a call to wake up to something that needs attention. I'm being asked to respond in a new way."

Rachel adds. "Yes, like my nightmare about the foods catching on fire. That dream pushes me to get out and change old eating habits."

"So, the wakeup call signals the imperative to journey out into the unknown," Sam says, picking up the thread. "In dreams, just as in waking life, embarking into the unknown is a major theme. Crisis strikes. For all of us in this room, cancer struck. Life has launched us into the journey."

Amy adds, "It's a ticket to someplace else."

Sam continues, "For me, the healing journey is much like the classic 'Hero's Journey' so aptly described by Joseph Campbell several years ago.[6] Many others have called it the mythic journey. Stages of this archetypal experience make up the basic plot for countless books and movies. First comes the 'call'; then the journeyer steps into the unknown. Next the seeker meets barriers and pitfalls and all sorts of obstacles. The journeyer also meets helpers and guides. After many trials and tribulations, the journeyer prevails, finally finds the treasure, or in some way achieves the goal of the journey. Then the Hero returns, determined to share whatever has been gained from the journey."

Sam pauses and Jay speaks, "Dreams are full of journey imagery. In my dreams I'm challenged by one 'monster' after another. The monsters are my shadow energies. I wrestle with them. I'm blocked by one obstacle after another. I descend into the depths and ascend incredible heights. Allies come to help me. In my dreams, I slowly become more creative and less fearful in my responses. I more easily allow support. I get closer and closer to 'the treasure.'"

The group is quiet. Laura asks, "What is the 'treasure' that you seek? What is the 'treasure' that you find?"

Jay answers, "At the beginning of the cancer journey, I was seeking a cure. Once I got into the mind-body practices, particularly dream appreciation, I found I was discovering new ways to live a larger life. I wanted to keep seeking more and more of what I was already finding. For me, the journey itself has become the treasure."

Emily stirs in her seat. "I'm thinking about the power company workers in hard hats who arrived in my ice storm dream. For me, they're images of mysterious inner support that always shows up. For me, the treasure is my growing trust in this mystery."

Margaret adds, "There are so many treasures, so many gifts. For me, Emily's hard hat workers are an example of the gift of humor. Where do these wacky images come from? Think of the clever metaphors, the amazing puns. I feel that many times, my dreams are simply asking me to lighten up and laugh. Humor and laughter have such a positive effect on the immune system.[7] Think of how often we laugh in this group."

Margaret continues, "In so many of my dreams, there is the theme of wandering and losing my way. In others I'm finding a new path, finding a new room in my house, discovering a beautiful garden. In my dreams, the path of the journey is a spiral. The main theme seems to be the eternal spiral of life, death, and then new life. It's a spiral of having, losing, and finding something new. For me, working with dreams and imagery has become a way of living, dying, and finding new life on levels far beyond the level of literal interpretation. And this is a great treasure when you're facing illness."

Laura glances down at the recorder. "Thank you, Margaret. I'm so grateful for all the reflections today. Perhaps we can close with comments you might make to anyone who is thinking about beginning a relationship with dream appreciation and guided imagery? What do you think is important to add?"

Jay responds, "We all dream. But if you don't think you remember your dreams, you can start writing down emotionally charged waking events. You can use dream appreciation questions and work with waking experiences as if they are dreams. Also, you can ask for healing waking dreams through guided imagery. If you do this, I can almost guarantee you that you'll find insight for living, and that that you'll also start remembering night dreams."

"And when you do remember your dreams," Rachel says, "you'll find that one image can be more impactful than a mouth full of words. Dreams bring you just the imagery you need—sometimes to soothe you, sometimes to light a fire under you."

"Don't get into relationship with dreams and imagery unless you really want to change," Emily says quietly. "Meeting the shadow and slowly forming new relationship to all the challenges in life is very hard. But the supportive energy for developing new perceptions, attitudes, and beliefs is always present."

Amy has been trying to remember what has already been said. She adds, "An important part of my dream-appreciation practice is that I direct my imagery as healing energy both inward to my body and mind and outward to others and beyond. Directing the energy feels to me like directing the paint on my paintbrush or smoothing an area of clay sculpture. I feel connected to creative spirit."

Sam says, "Expanding on Amy's idea about directing the energy of imagery, it's important to emphasize that our imagery affects our physiology. There is a lot of research that shows the positive effects of imagery on the body's healing systems. [8] We also know that dreams bring highly targeted imagery for keeping our bodies and minds in balance.[9]

"One more comment," Margaret says. "Through my dream-work practice with guided imagery, I know I've grown in compassion—toward newly discovered parts of myself, toward neglected parts of myself, toward other people, toward inner and outer life situations. Also, I've gained a renewed sense of meaning and purpose in my life. I hope that more and more people will open themselves to explore this practice. I hope that that more people come to find the countless gifts that dreams and guided imagery so freely give."

Laura looks around the circle, smiles, and says, "Thank you. Let's sit quietly for a few moments before we close our session.

"Closing your eyes, if you like . . . Breathing in, renewing . . . Breathing out, releasing . . . Moving down into a deeply centered place within . . . With each breath, renewing, relaxing, releasing . . . Inviting an image of Supportive Presence . . . Breathing in sustenance for the journey into wholeness and larger life.

YOUR OWN REFLECTIONS

1. As you continue your journey, what is the treasure you seek? What are some of the treasures you already have found?

2. Begin to notice when your dreams might be inviting you to lighten up. Sometimes you might feel the humor while you are still in the dream. More often, you will probably catch the puns, the cartoon-nature of the images, the "jokes" as you are writing the dream down. Dreams function to help bring balance to mind, body, and spirit. It is as if dreams often are trying to say, "Don't forget to enjoy!" Make a note whenever you receive an invitation.

3. Close your eyes. Breathe and relax into a deep meditative space. Imagine that you are the heroine or hero in the midst of a mythic journey. Invite an image of a challenge you are currently facing. Allow time for the imagery to develop. Invite an image of an ally who will help you. Allow time to savor feelings of support. Remaining in a meditative space, begin to write about the experience in your journal.

4. If you are a caregiver or health professional, your willingness to listen with empathy and compassion is part of the treasure you will find, both for yourself and for the other.

SCRIPT I
GUIDED IMAGERY FOR DEEP RELAXATION

You may want to record this script for deep relaxation or to ask someone you trust to read it to you. You can also download it with background music from our website. When you have become familiar with the steps of the practice, you may want to play your own choice of background music and conduct your own inner journey without a script. If at any time you become uncomfortable while listening, stop and open your eyes. You may find that unexpected issues and emotions arise and that you want to discontinue. Simply open your eyes and focus once more on your breathing. You are in charge of the process at all times. Please do not ever move into a meditative state while driving.

Begin by closing your eyes if that's comfortable . . . whether sitting or lying down, aligning your body so energy can flow freely . . . breathing naturally while moving your attention inside . . . connecting with the breath . . . renewing with each inhale . . . releasing with each exhale . . . breathing in . . . breathing out . . . drawing in the warm energy of renewal . . . and with each out-breath, releasing whatever needs to be released . . . breath moving in . . . breath moving out . . . with each breath relaxing deeper and deeper into a centered place within . . . all the inner fragments becoming still and quiet . . .

Now checking in with your body . . . sending the warm energy of the breath to any place that needs special care . . . moving your focus to your toes . . . allowing your toes to relax . . . all ten toes . . .

and moving your attention through your feet . . . allowing both feet to soften and relax . . . and moving attention through your ankles . . . and through your lower legs . . . your knees . . . your thighs . . . and into your buttocks and hips . . . sinking more deeply into the support of whatever you're sitting or lying on . . . and now checking in with your trunk . . . breathing into the pelvic region . . . bringing in the breath of renewal . . . releasing whatever is needing to be released . . . and into your abdomen . . . up through your solar plexus . . . into your chest . . . your heart . . . your lungs . . . with each breath, filling with renewal all the way up to your collar bones . . . and releasing whatever needs to be released . . .

Now moving your attention around the sides of your body and into your back . . . breathing into your lower back from your tail bone . . . through the sacrum . . . your lower back . . . mid back . . . into your upper back . . . noticing your shoulder blades and the space between your shoulder blades . . . and now your shoulders and down through your arms and hands . . . noticing both hands . . . your fingers and thumbs . . . your palms and the backs of your hands . . . and through your wrists . . . lower arms . . . elbows . . . upper arms and back into your shoulders . . . and now checking in with your neck . . . breathing in warmth and renewal . . allowing any place that needs tending to loosen and soften . . . all through your neck and throat relaxing, releasing . . . and now noticing your head . . . allowing the back of your scalp to relax . . . all across the top of your scalp . . . your forehead . . . all around your eyes . . . your cheeks . . . all around your mouth . . . your chin . . . your eyes heavy in their sockets . . . your tongue soft and heavy in your mouth . . . noticing your entire body.

Breathing in, renewing . . . breathing out, releasing, relaxing . . . moving into a deeply centered place within . . . resting in a place of deep harmony and balance at the center of your being . . . ready now to connect with your dream . . . .

You may download this script from:
www.healingpowerofdreams.com

SCRIPT II
GUIDED IMAGERY FOR NIGHTMARE TRANSFORMATION

You may want to record this script for dream re-entry or to ask someone you trust to read it to you. You can also download it with background music from our website. When you have become familiar with the steps of the practice, you may want to play your own choice of background music and conduct your own inner journey without a script. If at any time you become uncomfortable while listening, stop and open your eyes. You may find that unexpected issues and emotions arise and that you want to discontinue. Simply open your eyes and focus once more on your breathing. You are in charge of the process at all times. Please do not ever move into a meditative state while driving.

Once again, moving back into meditative space with the intention to heal your nightmare experience . . . arranging your body to allow energy to flow freely . . . closing your eyes . . . and once again moving your attention inside and connecting with your breath . . . breathing in, renewing . . . breathing out, releasing . . . moving down into deep relaxation . . . allowing your mind and your emotions to become still and quiet, like fragments in a kaleidoscope settling into a restful design . . . and with each breath relaxing, releasing, and moving deeper and deeper down, down into a centered place within . . . feeling calm, feeling peaceful . . .

Checking in with your body . . . sending the warm energy of the breath to anyplace that needs special care . . . breathing in, renewing . . . breathing out, releasing, relaxing . . . moving down, down into a deep place of balance and a sense of wellbeing . . . breathing . . . relaxing . . . releasing . . . imagining the free flow of life energy moving through your body, perhaps as streams of light, perhaps streams of color . . . perhaps feeling the movement of sensations . . . vibrating molecules of life energy flowing unimpeded from your head to your toes . . . from your toes to your head . . . life energy nourishing every organ, every tissue, every tiny cell . . . and while the energy flows in balance and harmony . . .

Opening your imagination, and now moving into an inner sanctuary, your own unique healing place that feels completely safe and supportive . . . a place you may have been before, or a place you are seeing for the first time . . . opening all your senses . . . looking around, listening . . . taking in the atmosphere . . . feeling a sense of safety and wellbeing in your body . . . breathing in the energy of sanctuary and healing that is all around you . . . savoring every detail of this healing space . . .

And now inviting an image of supportive presence . . . feeling your heart open as you recognize you are not alone . . . feeling totally seen, totally understood . . . totally accepted by a companion or companions with you . . . opening your heart knowing that your experience is witnessed and shared . . . that you re-enter your dream in safety and with the certainty of support . . . feeling great strength and compassion with you . . .

So feeling firmly grounded in a sense of safety and support . . . slowly re-entering your dream with trust that the disturbing experience will shift and transform in a healing way . . .

First moving to a safe vantage point . . . observing the dream from a safe distance in the company of supportive presence . . . watching it from a new perspective, from a viewpoint of safety for as long as you like . . . totally present with all of your senses . . . viewing the dream with new lenses . . . watching for as long as you like . . . changing your perspective and distance from the dream as many times as you choose . . . feeling the support of whoever is with you . . .

Whenever you feel ready, you may slowly begin to interact with your dream . . . staying connected to the energy of your support . . . carefully moving into the experience only when you feel ready . . . initiating dialogue if you choose . . . staying grounded in a sense of safety . . .

Allowing the dream to move, to shift, to change . . . allowing yourself as dreamer to respond in new ways to whatever is happening . . . allowing yourself to be fully present . . . expressing new strengths, new attitudes . . . allowing both the images and the energies to flow . . . allowing the dream to become a new dream . . . allowing your new responses to transform the dream . . . allowing the new dream to touch your heart, your entire body, your mind, your spirit . . .staying with the new dream for as long as you like . . .

And when you feel ready to come back from this journey . . . turning to your supportive companion or companions . . . whoever has shared this experience with you . . . expressing gratitude . . . expressing appreciation for being with you and standing by . . .

And gathering up whatever you want to bring back from this journey . . . now slowly beginning to return to waking consciousness . . . knowing that you can return to an inner sanctuary whenever you choose . . . you can be in the company of supportive presence . . . you can re-enter your ever-transforming dream . . . you can respond and express yourself in new ways, allowing the new dream to act as good dream medicine in all the parts of your life that need healing . . .

Slowly coming back . . . beginning to move your fingers and toes . . . very slowly opening your eyes . . . now fully awake . . . ready now to record the experience . . . knowing that every time you go inward to engage in healing work . . . you nourish your body . . . you nourish your mind . . . you nourish your spirit . . .

You may download this script from:
www.healingpowerofdreams.com

Script III
Guided Imagery for Inviting a Healing
Waking Dream

You may want to record this script for inviting a healing waking dream or to ask someone you trust to read it to you. You can also download it with background music from our website. When you have become familiar with the steps of the practice, you may want to play your own choice of background music and conduct your own inner journey without a script. If at any time you become uncomfortable while listening, stop and open your eyes. You may find that unexpected issues and emotions arise and that you want to discontinue. Simply open your eyes and focus once more on your breathing. You are in charge of the process at all times. Please do not ever move into a meditative state while driving.

Begin by closing your eyes if that's comfortable . . . whether sitting or lying down, aligning your body so energy can flow . . . beginning to breathe and relax into a deep, centered, meditative space. Inhaling . . . renewing . . . exhaling . . . releasing . . . with each breath letting go anything that needs to be let go . . . progressively relaxing each part of your body . . . renewing . . . releasing . . . relaxing . . .

Noticing where you are holding tension . . . sending the warm energy of the breath to soothe and soften anyplace that needs to relax . . . acknowledging where you might be feeling a bit off balance . . . imagining little fragments coming together into a beautiful design . . .

allowing your thoughts and emotions to become still and quiet . . . sinking deeper and deeper into a centered place within . . .

Using all your senses . . . now imagining one of your inner sanctuary abodes . . . settling into one of your unique healing places . . . becoming totally present . . . taking in the atmosphere . . . allowing the energy of this place to impact your body, mind, and soul.

Now, inviting Supportive Presence to be with you . . . allowing an image of a loving companion or companions to come into your special place . . . savoring the energy of the image that arises . . . opening your heart to the presence that comes . . .

Safe and centered in your special healing place . . . in the company of compassionate support . . . now, inviting a "waking dream," an experience from the realm of imagination intended to bring about imagery that will help you further your healing and growth . . .

Opening to receive whatever experience comes . . . giving the imagery time to develop . . . using all your senses . . . being fully present to whatever experience comes to you . . .

Suspending judgment . . . staying open to the moment . . . entering into dialogue with a symbol from the dream if that feels appropriate . . . including your Supportive Presence in the dialogue if you like . . .

Concluding your interaction whenever you choose . . . hoping to have at least one clear experience to bring back . . . and whether you understand the waking dream or not, expressing gratitude for the power of the imagination and for the presence of support . . .

Making a mental note of what you want to bring back from the waking dream . . . trusting that it has come from a deep level of consciousness . . . and carries insight and energy for healing . . . trusting the mystery . . .

Knowing that you can return to your waking dream whenever you choose . . . you can re-enter this same dream and allow it to develop . . . or, you may keep seeking a new healing waking dream until you reach a felt-experience of new relationship with before-unexplored aspects of your life . . .

Now slowly beginning to return to ordinary waking consciousness . . . and still maintaining a state of reverie, quickly writing down your experience with the intention to explore this meditative dream at a later time with symbol appreciation questions . . . knowing that every time you set aside time to explore your inner journeys . . . you nourish your body . . . you nourish your mind . . . you nourish your spirit.

You may download this script from:

www.healingpowerofdreams.com

Script IV
Guided Imagery for Integrating Healing Symbols

You may want to record this script for integrating healing imagery or to ask someone you trust to read it to you. You can also download it with background music from our website. When you have become familiar with the steps of the practice, you may want to play your own choice of background music and conduct your own inner journey without a script. If at any time you become uncomfortable while listening, stop and open your eyes. You may find that unexpected issues and emotions arise and that you want to discontinue. Simply open your eyes and focus once more on your breathing. You are in charge of the process at all times. Please do not ever move into a meditative state while driving.

Once again, moving back into meditative space with the intention to bring in energy that can impact your body, mind and spirit in a healing way . . . arranging your body to allow energy to flow freely . . . closing your eyes . . . and again moving your attention inside and connecting with your breath . . . breathing in, renewing . . . breathing out, releasing . . . with each breath moving down into deep relaxation . . . allowing your mind and your emotions to become still and quiet . . . like fragments in a kaleidoscope settling into a restful design . . . and with each breath relaxing, releasing, and moving deeper and deeper down, down into a centered place within . . . feeling calm, feeling peaceful . . .

Checking in with your body . . . sending the warm energy of the breath to anyplace that needs special care . . . breathing in, renewing . . . breathing out, releasing, relaxing . . . moving down, down into a deep place of balance and a sense of wellbeing . . . breathing . . . relaxing . . . releasing.

Opening your imagination, and now moving into an inner sanctuary . . . your own unique healing place that feels completely safe and supportive . . . a place you may have been before, or a place you are seeing for the first time . . . opening all your senses . . . looking around, listening . . . taking in the atmosphere . . . feeling a sense of safety and wellbeing in your body . . . breathing in the energy of sanctuary and healing that is all around you . . . savoring every detail of this healing space . . .

And now inviting an image of supportive presence . . . feeling your heart open as you recognize you are not alone . . . feeling totally seen, totally understood . . . totally accepted by a companion or companions with you . . . opening your heart knowing that your experience is witnessed and shared . . . that you are in a place of safety and certainty of support . . . feeling great strength and compassion with you . . .

Inviting now one of your healing symbols . . . allowing the image to become so vivid that it begins to seem realer than real . . . if the symbol begins to change, allowing change to happen . . . trusting deep wisdom to shape the image for this particular time . . . allowing plenty of time . . .

Now savoring the energy of your symbol . . . allowing the image to turn into a free flow of life energy moving through your body, perhaps as streams of light, perhaps streams of color . . . perhaps feeling the movement of sensations . . . vibrating molecules of life energy flowing unimpeded from your head to your toes . . . from your toes to your head . . . life energy nourishing every organ, every tissue, every tiny cell . . . and while the energy flows in balance and harmony . . . if there is a particular place in your body that needs special tending . . . focusing the energy into that area . . . perhaps placing your hands on that area of your body and imagining the light coming through your hands to surround and penetrate . . . if you cannot place your hands on the area, simply focusing the light with your mind and heart . . . directing the energy of healing imagery into your body.

And for any time of mental and emotional turmoil, allowing the flow of light and life energy to sweep through your mind and heart . . . clearing away the clutter . . . smoothing the rocky pathway . . . calming the crashing waves . . . bringing the collage of clashing colors into a harmonious design . . . bringing a sense of spacious stillness . . . and with each breath, moving down, down, into this centered place of stillness. Savoring the silence . . . resting in a sense of peace and calm.

And when longing for spiritual connection . . . focusing on your yearning . . . yearning for relationship with power and support that is greater than yourself . . . allowing the energy of your healing imagery to take you across the bridge into a realm of great spirit and mystery . . . walking across the bridge into the place that has always been your home . . . opening all your senses . . . allowing your heart to be filled with light . . . allowing your soul to be filled . . . breathing in the energy of gratitude . . . breathing out the energy of blessing.

And when wanting to send out healing energy to others . . . gathering the light of your healing image into your heart . . . with each breath, allowing your sense of compassion and blessing to grow . . . light expanding with each in-breath . . . light intensifying with each out-breath . . . and from your heart . . . directing the light outward to specific others or situations or issues that you are wanting to touch . . . and when you choose, perhaps sending out to others that you do not know, or to others who have hurt you, or to unknown situations and issues in this world and beyond . . . breathing in the energy of gratitude . . . breathing out the energy of blessing.

You may download this script from:
www.healingpowerofdreams.com

WORKSHEET 1
SYMBOL APPRECIATION QUESTIONS

Choose a symbol from your dream. It can be a response, interaction, person, animal or object. Write as quickly as you can without censoring. If you write quickly, you will more readily express metaphoric phrases that will help you intuit connection to your waking life.

1. Describe your symbol as if for someone who has no concept of what it is.

2. What is the function, the purpose of your symbol, particularly in the dream?

3. What are your associations to the symbol?

4. What memories does it stir?

5. What do you like and dislike about this symbol?

6. What do you feel in your body as you reflect on the symbol?

7. How are you responding or interacting with the symbol? Is anyone else in the dream responding in a different way?

8. How is this symbol a bridge to your waking life? Where or when in your life did you or do you feel the same as you feel with this symbol? Do any of your associations to the symbol resonate as metaphors for waking life?

9. What insights does the symbol bring? Does it help you to identify a perception, belief, attitude, or pattern of behavior you might need to release or one you might need to claim and integrate in order to move into an expanded way of being?

10. How can you honor this symbol by bringing its insights and energies into your waking life?

Worksheet 2
Six "Magic" Questions

Appreciation to Robert J. Hoss for permission to offer part of an exercise that he presents in his book *Dream Language: Self Understanding through Imagery and Color*. Hoss distilled the questions from Fritz Perl's Gestalt method of dream work. The six questions allow symbols in the dream to have a voice and to speak for themselves. (Members of Cancer Project dream circles try to downshift into a meditative state before doing the exercise; and we ask they not do the exercise with a person they actually know.)

- Choose any dream symbol that draws your attention.

- Let the image answer in its own voice. Record the responses in the present tense.

1. As the image, who or what are you? (Name and freely describe yourself and perhaps how you feel as the dream image.) "I am____ and I feel____.

2. As the image, what is your purpose or function? What do you do? "My purpose is to ____."

3. As the dream image, what do you like about who you are and what you do? "I like____."

4. As the dream image, what do you dislike about who you are and what you do? "I dislike____."

5. As the dream image, what do you fear most? "I fear____."

6. As the dream image, what do you desire most? "I desire____."

(Added by IASD cancer dream groups: What did you come to teach me?)

"Relate to waking life: Do one or more of the statements sound like a way you feel, or a situation in your waking life? Do the 'I am' and 'My purpose' statements sound like a role you are playing in waking life? Do the 'I like' versus the 'I dislike' statements sound like a conflict going on inside you? Do the 'I fear' and the 'I desire' statements sound like waking life fears and desires, perhaps feeding the conflict? If the dream character is someone you know, does some aspect of the character's personality relate to a manner in which you are approaching the waking life situation, or alternatively, does this dream character have a personality trait that your admire or wish you had more of in order to better handle this waking life situation?" (Hoss, 214.)

WORKSHEET 3
MY HEALING IMAGERY

Please date the images that you list so that you can later review them in your journal. Note recurring imagery. Use these symbols in self-guided imagery exercises to nourish mind, body, and spirit.

- My special sanctuaries for healing work:

- Images of Supportive Presence:

- Settings from dreams that bring a sense of peace and calm:

- Surprises in dreams that help me change direction:

- Situations that evoke a sense of renewal and hope:

- Characters and experiences that bring a sense of guidance:

- Characteristics in dream characters that you feel are totally missing in yourself: (Might a tiny bit of this energy help in your healing process?)

- Transformed imagery through a series of dreams:

- "Numinous" encounters that evoke a sense of awe and wonder:

Appendix I:
Dream Group Guidelines and Process

Dream circles in integrative wellness centers are by nature slightly different from dream groups in other settings. In wellness facilities, the dream circle is sometimes designated a stress reduction class, and new participants can begin at any time and are not expected to commit to consistent attendance. Sessions are short: an hour and a half instead of the two to three hours often allotted for dream sharing in other settings. Some dream circles meet each week, but some are scheduled for once or twice a month.

Underlying principles for group dream sharing are based on the work of Montague Ullman and Jeremy Taylor.

Montague Ullman (1916-2008) was a psychiatrist, psychoanalyst, and parapsychologist who founded the Dream Laboratory at Maimonides Medical Center in Brooklyn, NY. For over three decades he actively promoted interest in dreams and in sharing dreams in a group. Safety of the dreamer was all important to his approach.

Montague Ullman and Nan Zimmerman, *Working With Dreams* (New York, Dellecorte Press, 1979).

Jeremy Taylor is the author of four books that have been translated into many languages. His latest book is *The Wisdom of Your Dreams: Using Dreams to Tap Into Your Unconscious and Transform Your Life.*

He is an ordained Unitarian Universalist minister, has worked with dreams and has facilitated dream group sharing for over forty years. In his approach, he blends "the values of spirituality with an active social conscience and a Jungian perspective." (Anon.)

Jeremy Taylor, *Dream Work: Techniques for Discovering the Creative Power in Dreams* (New York, Paulist Press,1983).

While maintaining their basic principles, our process continues to evolve.

1. Dreams speak the universal language of symbol and metaphor.

2. For every dream, there are multiple meanings, and each person in the group may find several meanings in any dream that is shared.

3. The dreamer is the only one who can say what the dream means to him or her. A sense of inner resonance, a sense of "aha," is the only measure of validity for the dreamer.

4. Reflections from other circle members enhance possibilities for the dreamer's broader understanding and also provide an opportunity for each person in the group to engage in inner work.

5. When a dream is shared within the circle, the dreamer is in charge at all times and may always choose how much or how little to say. The dreamer may close the discussion at any time.

6. For group work, recent dreams are preferable to old dreams unless the dream is a recurring dream. Short dreams are preferable to long dreams.

7. When offering reflections about someone else's dream, group members speak of their own experiences. They are not interpreting the dream for the dreamer, but instead are sharing reflections about their own inner dynamics that get activated by hearing the dream. They **project** their own associations, memories, and concepts onto the dream, prefacing their remarks with "If it were my dream . . ." or "In my dream . . . ." In this way, each person in the circle can learn about her or his own inner dynamics, and the dreamer can hear new insights that may or may not resonate.

8. Respect, appreciation, and wonder are the three main attitudes needed for group sharing.

Goals for the Facilitator:

1. Provide a safe, supportive container, facilitating confidentiality regarding all personal information. If the dreamer gives permission, dreams may be retold outside the group with the dreamer remaining anonymous. All dream circles in the Cancer Project adhere to the IASD Ethics Statement which is designed to safeguard the dreamer (see Appendix 2).

2. Teach and facilitate basic dream-group guidelines, basic dream appreciation techniques, basic guided imagery techniques, and approaches for continuing to embody and integrate healing energies beyond the group setting.

3. Model and facilitate attitudes of appreciation, wonder, deep listening, openness, and non-judgment.

Model and help everyone understand that the dream circle is a place where each member can feel supported in discovering strength and new possibilities, not a place for "fixing" concerns and conflicts.

PROCESS

Set Up: Members meet in a space that provides privacy. The facilitator arranges the chairs in a circle and sometimes lights a candle in the center. Fire rules dictate that most wellness centers use battery powered candles. Some groups like to bring personally meaningful items, poems, or art work to be placed in the center of the circle.

Introductions: When a new participant comes, the facilitator extends welcome and asks each person in the circle to say his or her name and briefly state their reason for attending the wellness center. The facilitator offers new participants a handbook, *The Healing Power of Dreams and Nightmares*, to take home after the meeting and assures them the process will be explained as the group moves through the experience.

(*Healing Power of Dreams Manual*: Written in 2005 by Tallulah Lyons and Wendy Pannier for the IASD Cancer Project. Each dream group and workshop participant receives a copy. A manual for facilitators is also available).

Opening Ritual: After introductions, the facilitator reminds members of the requirement of confidentiality and either asks for a few moments of silence or leads a short guided imagery exercise to center into a deeper layer of consciousness. The opening ritual marks transition from the outer to the inner world, from literal to symbolic thinking, from the known world into mystery. Through silence or guided imagery, dreamers can reconnect with the dreams brought for sharing. Examples of opening meditations are found in the text.

Check In: Each person checks in with brief comments on his or her emotional state and on what might be contributing to the emotions. This is not a time to go into lengthy descriptions of outer life events. Example: "I'm feeling pretty down because my counts are low again, but I'm feeling glad because my daughter is coming next month." The facilitator gently delays any discussion and questions. Time is limited and getting to the dreams is top priority.

Dream Gathering: After check in, it is time to gather the dreams. If there are only three or four present in the group, the first person gives the title of a dream, names the primary emotions, and immediately proceeds to read or tell the dream. The next person then gives a title, the emotions, and reads a dream. Anyone may pass, and anyone may offer a "waking dream" instead of a sleeping dream. (Review Chapter 9) **This is dream gathering time, so we still want to delay questions and comments.**

- If more than four people are present, instead of reading an entire dream, each person simply gives the title and primary feelings of a dream.

- If new people are present, they are invited to read or tell a dream, or to tell the group about their experience with dreams, and to say what questions they have and what they hope to find in the group. There is still no discussion so that the group can move on to dream sharing as quickly as possible.

Choosing a Dream: Unless a new person has come in with a burning desire to share a dream, the choice is based on the intensity of the dreams that have been presented and the needs of a person who has not had a recent turn. Nightmares take top priority, provided the dreamer wants to share. If someone asks to share, we try to honor the request. If several want to share, the facilitator can write the titles on slips of paper and draw lots, trusting synchronicity.

Re-centering: Before the dreamer reads or tells the selected dream again, group members are asked to re-center, to drop into meditative space so that they can listen deeply. We allow a few seconds for silence.

Dream reading or telling: Very slowly, the dreamer tells or reads the dream without interruption. Dreamers are asked to **use the present tense** to create a sense of immediacy, but if use of present tense proves difficult for the presenter, past tense will do. The facilitator can model the use of present tense during the projection time. At some point, the facilitator wants to teach the use of present tense to new participants, but not at the expense of interrupting the meditative flow.

The group listens while maintaining a meditative state. Each person's intention is to hear the dream as her or his own experience, to feel the emotions as her or his own. If time allows, the dreamer reads or tells the dream again. If the dreamer agrees, others may take notes. Note taking helps many people to process, but the notes are always offered to the dreamer at the end of the session.

Clarifying Questions: Members ask questions to clarify emotions, then to clarify details of the settings and plot such as ages, colors, times of day, directions, sizes, textures, types, quantities, etc. **This is not the time to ask for the dreamer's associations or links to waking life.** If the dreamer spontaneously comments on associations or meanings, other members forgo asking for elaboration and do not ask why the dreamer feels a certain way. Feelings and meanings are to be acknowledged and respected, not questioned or debated.

The dreamer's associations and links to waking life will be shared later. This is a deliberate choice that reduces the questioning time and allows participants to project onto the dream more of their own inner dynamics than if they had been told the dreamer's associations and past history. Minimizing personal questions offers protection for the dreamer, and is very important in groups that are open to new participants at every session.

Projections: After answering clarifying questions, the dreamer turns the dream over to the group. Circle members now have a chance to "project" their reflections onto the dream. The facilitator suggests that the dreamer take notes and not look at the others during the projection time. The dreamer's looking down, listening, and writing helps the others to remember that they are not interpreting the dream for the dreamer but are, indeed, talking about how the dream affects them personally.

Members now talk with one another and avoid asking any more questions of the dreamer. Members always preface their remarks with "In my dream . . . If it were my dream . . . In my imagined version of the dream." Dreamers are sharing their own inner dynamics in the same way they might talk about how a work of art is affecting them. They are speaking of their own associations and memories triggered by the dream. They are not interpreting the dream for the dreamer, though we hope the dreamer is receiving new insights and possibilities from the discussion.

Back to the Dreamer: After group projections, the dream is "given back" to the dreamer, who is free to say or not say anything more about the dream or about the group's projections. At this point the dreamer may choose to offer or not offer associations and waking-life links to some of the main symbols and interactions in the dream. **Circle members listen with empathy but do not question the dreamer's remarks, offer "fixes," or tell the dreamer what the dream means.**

Exploring gifts for integration: After the dreamer's comments, it is time to identify possible insights of the dream and to create possibilities for integrating the gifts. The dreamer takes the lead, if he or she chooses. The dreamer begins to ponder what this dream might be trying to offer and how the new energies can be integrated. Others join in with suggestions for how they might embody and integrate the dream **for themselves** "if it were their dream." They discuss meditative and active imagination practices they might use as well as concrete and doable small actions that might personally help them to manifest the insights and energies of the dream. **It is inappropriate for anyone to suggest ways to "fix" the dreamer's concerns or conflicts.**

Ideally, everyone in the group now feels a bit of insight and new energy. Ideally, there is time to explore one more dream.

Realistically, however, there is usually a new person who has many questions. Also regular members often prefer to focus on their own dream of the day rather than explore another dream in depth. Doctors' appointments and medical treatments interrupt consistent attendance in the circle, so whenever a member can attend, she or he is often glad to ask and discuss personal dream questions.

Final Round: We go around the circle again. This time, each person gives the title of a dream and then talks briefly about evocative imagery that can become the focus of their own meditative practice, ongoing dialogue, or small actions such as those discussed in Chapter 10. Each person has a chance to reconnect with imagery and energy of his or her own dream to carry into the week.

Closing Ritual: To close, the group stands in a circle. This can be a time for silence or for the facilitator to express gratitude, naming the images that have come as gifts to the circle, or for circle members to speak their own gratitude if they wish. The ritual can be a time to give expression to the hope of integrating gifts of the dreams into the healing journey. Examples of closing rituals can be found in the text.

There are many ways to conduct a dream circle, but the above process is one that has proved to be safe and effective with IASD cancer groups. Within the guidelines of each particular wellness center and the guidelines offered above, each facilitator offers a personal style that assures the process remain flexible. Some groups spend the most time on the projective work; some spend more time on guided imagery exercises. In wellness centers, all dreamers are encouraged to integrate their work through practices in other classes—guided imagery, meditation, journaling, yoga, qui gong, tai chi, drumming, music, and all the expressive arts.

Appendix II
IASD Ethics Statement

The International Association for the Study of Dreams (IASD) celebrates the many benefits of dream work, yet recognizes that there are potential risks. IASD supports an approach to dream work and dream sharing that respects the dreamer's dignity and integrity, and which recognizes the dreamer as the decision-maker regarding the significance of the dream. Systems of dream work that assign authority or knowledge of the dream's meanings to someone other than the dreamer can be misleading, incorrect, and harmful. Ethical dream work helps the dreamer to more fully experience, appreciate, and understand the dream. Every dream may have multiple meanings, and different techniques may be reasonably employed to touch these multiple layers of significance.

A dreamer's decision to share or discontinue sharing a dream should always be respected and honored. The dreamer should be forewarned that unexpected issues or emotions may arise in the course of the dream work. Information and mutual agreement about the degree of privacy and confidentiality are essential ingredients in creating a safe atmosphere for dream sharing. Dream work outside a clinical setting is not a substitute for psychotherapy, or other professional treatment, and should not be used as such.

IASD recognizes and respects that there are many valid and time-honored dream work traditions. We invite and welcome the participation of dreamers from all cultures. There are social, cultural, and transpersonal aspects to dream experience. In this statement, we do not mean to imply that the only valid approach to dream work focuses on the dreamer's personal life. Our purpose is to honor and respect the person of the dreamer as well as the dream itself, regardless of how the relationship between the two may be understood.

Note: All dream work in workshops and ongoing dream groups of the IASD cancer project adhere to this Ethics Statement and put the safety of the dreamer as a top priority

APPENDIX III:
BENEFITS OF WORKING WITH DREAMS

BODY

Dreaming is a natural process that helps to maintain health and wellbeing. During sleep and dreaming, the body conserves energy so that it can refresh and repair. Sleeping and dreaming play critical roles in the development of memory and learning. Dreaming and working with dreams help to create new connections and networks in the brain that can lead to expanded living.

- Dreams sometimes predict illness, allowing the dreamer to seek early diagnosis and treatment.

- Dreams often offer guidance concerning lifestyle and treatment options.

- Dream imagery that has been experienced as healing to the dreamer can be directed through guided imagery to soothe specific places in the body.

MIND

- Dreams highlight inner conflicts that produce hidden stress. Dream work is one of the best ways to identify, analyze, and engage with fear, anger, loss of control, sense of isolation, and other attitudes and emotions that produce stress and inhibit immune functioning.

- Working with dreams enlarges a sense of inner authority and strengthens a sense of focus and direction for the recovery process.

- Dreams provide a safe place to experience every kind of emotion. They offer new possibilities for creative expression of emotion in waking life. With dream work, energy can be freed from repression and projection and directed toward living with a sense of renewal and connection.

- The dreams of those facing cancer often re-activate past personal trauma and use past experiences in symbolic ways to remind the dreamer of enduring strengths and capacities for moving through illness and future crisis.

- Many dreams, particularly when shared, produce laughter. It has long been shown that laughter is good not only for the mind but also for the immune system.

- Dream imagery that has been experienced as healing to the dreamer can be directed through guided imagery to help transform emotional issues.

SPIRIT

- Working with dreams strengthens conscious participation with deep creative energy that inspires and empowers the dreamer to live life to the fullest.

- People who work with dreams over time, report finding a sense of meaning and purpose, a sense of deeper relationship with themselves and others.

- People who work with dreams over time, report a sense of connection with "mystery" beyond the conscious ego.

- Dream imagery that has been experienced as healing to the dreamer can be re-experienced through guided imagery to enhance a sense of spiritual connection.

RESEARCH

IASD Yearly Cancer Project Survey, (Pannier and Lyons). Since 2005, in an informal survey based on a quality of life survey from The Wellness Community, the majority of participants in ongoing dream groups report

- Decreased feelings of anxiety and stress.

- Increased sense of connection with others.

- Increased sense of connection to inner resources.

- Increased understanding of healing at multiple levels.

- Increased sense of quality of life—particularly emotional, social, and spiritual.

- Increased feelings of confidence and control over life and health issues.

- Increased feelings of hope.

- Increased understanding of how to live fully now, despite cancer.

Recent research on the dreaming brain and the contributions of sleep and dreaming for health and well-being are summarized by dream expert Robert J. Hoss in *Dream Language: Self Understanding through Imagery and Color* (Ashland, OR: Innersource, 2005), with updates appearing regulary on his website www.dreamscience.org.

Based on numerous studies with thousands of dreams, dream researcher, Earnest Hartmann, M.D., concludes that dreams provide "exclamatory" metaphors for the dreamer's primary emotional concerns, and that they function to help make neuronal connections, not only to related emotional memories, but also to new possibilities. Ernest Hartmann, M.D. *Dreams and Nightmares.* New York: Perseus Book Group, 2001. Updates appear regularly on his website, web. me.com/ernesthartmann

Bestselling author, psychiatrist, and psychoanalyst Norman Doidge, M.D., discusses the requirement of REM sleep for the plastic development of the brain. He also discusses the progression of positive imagery and emotions in dreams as an indicator of the brain's remarkable power to unlearn certain associations and change existing synaptic connections to make way for new learning. Norman Doidge, M.D. *The Brain that Changes Itself.* New York: Penguin Books, 2007), 215-244.

Discussions of dreams as indicators of disturbances in the body are found in many sources:

Robert L. Van de Castle highlights the research of Russian psychiatrist, Vasily Kasakin and sites other proponents of diagnostic dreams. *Our Dreaming Mind.* New York: Ballantine Books, 1994, 361-370.

Patricia Garfield speaks of dreams that predict illness. *Healing Power of Dreams.* New York: Simon and Schuster, 1991.

Jeremy Taylor says, "There is . . . an aspect of every dream that provides an exquisitely accurate 'readout' of your physical health and condition of your body at the moment of the dream." *The Wisdom of Your Dreams.* New York: Tarcher/Penguin, 2009, 10.

Candace B. Pert, Ph.D., discusses the importance of dreams and says they "are direct messages from your bodymind, giving you valuable information about what's going on physiologically as well as emotionally." *Molecules of Emotions: The Science Behind Mind-Body Medicine.* New York: Simon and Schuster, 1997, 290-292.

APPENDIX IV:
BENEFITS OF RELAXATION/GUIDED IMAGERY

BODY

The Relaxation Response is a universal human capacity for reducing stress. It was researched by Herbert Benson, M.D., at Harvard Medical School in the sixties and is at the core of most meditative practices. The Relaxation Response is a relaxed, yet focused state of consciousness that brings about conditions in the body that are the exact opposite from the bodily conditions associated with the Fight or Flight Response or Stress Response. All processes slow down: heart rate, breathing rate, brain wave patterns, rate of oxygen consumption, carbon monoxide elimination; as stress hormones subside, endorphins increase. Activity moves from the frontal cortex to areas of the brain that process associations, sensations, and emotions. The body conserves energy so that it can refresh and repair.

Guided imagery can help evoke the Relaxation Response and can then be used to:

- direct modulation of all physiologic control systems including the immune system,

- reduce pain,

- reduce insomnia,

- reduce side effects of treatment including fatigue and nausea,

- speed recovery from surgery. (For surgery patients, guided imagery CDs sometimes are paid for by insurance.)

MIND

Guided imagery can help you to:

- transform limited perceptions, limiting attitudes, and habitual patterns of behavior that are not conducive to healing and growth;

- get in touch with feelings and express emotions in constructive ways;

- understand and transform resistance and suffering;

- transform fear and a sense of hopelessness into courage and a sense of hope;

- transform a sense of conflict into a sense of resolution and new possibilities; and

- develop a positive sense of self with a clear sense of goals and how to move toward them.

SPIRIT

Guided imagery can help you to:

- get in touch with a sense of meaning and purpose; to get in touch with a sense of connection and belonging; and

- experience a sense of support and relationship with *Mystery, Inner Wisdom, Inner Healer,* or whatever one chooses to call that which is bigger than the conscious ego.

RESEARCH

The Relaxation Response, Herbert Benson, M.D., Harper Collins, New York, 1975 and 2000.

Integrative Oncology, Principles and Practice, edited by Matthew P. Mumber, (London and New York, Taylor and Francis, 2006).

Integrative Oncology, edited by Donald Abrams, M.D., and Andrew Weil, M.D. (Oxford University Press, 2009).

Additional research on guided imagery for integrative healthcare is found on the websites of Belleruth Naparstek, www.healthjourneys.com, and Martin Rossman, M.D., www.thehealingmind.org.

Appendix V:
Recources

BOOKS ON DREAMS

Barasch, Marc Ian. **Healing Dreams: Exploring the Dreams that Can Change Your Life.** New York: Riverhead Books, 2001. (Barash's own dreams before diagnosis of thyroid cancer and his dreams of guidance throughout treatment.)

Bulkekey, Kelly. **Dreams of Healing: Transforming Nightmares into Visions of Hope.** New York: Paulist Press, 2003. (Written after 9/11. Dreams function to express turbulent emotions, work through confusion, heal psychic wounds, and creatively envision mew possibilities. Good research studies.)

Bulkeley, Kelly and Patricia Bulkley. **Dreaming Beyond Death: A Guide to Pre-Death Dreams and Visions.** Boston: Beacon Press, 2005. (Excellent resource for hospice workers.)

Burch, Wanda Easter. **She Who Dreams**. Novata, CA: New World Library, 2003. (Dreams and journey of a breast cancer survivor.)

Garfield, Patricia L. **The Healing Power of Dreams.** New York: Simon and Schuster, 1991. (A classic on dreams and healing. All of her books convey the healing nature of dreams and dream work.)

Gonglof, Robert. **Dream Exploration: A New Approach.** Woodbury, MN: Llewellyn Publishers, 2006. (How to discover the themes in your life and in your dreams.)

Gordon, David. **Mindful Dreaming**. Franklin Lakes, NJ: Career Press, 2006. (Dreams provide a compassionate and non-judgmental mirror. Approach contributes to mindfulness-based techniques now taught in most wellness centers.)

Haden, Robert L. **Unopened Letters from God**. Haden Institute Publishing, 2010. (A workbook for individuals and groups.)

Hartmann, Ernest. **Dreams and Nightmares: The Origin and Meaning of Dreams.** New York: Perseus Publishing, 1998. (Research shows that dreams, guided by emotions, make broad neuronal connections among our experiences in life and provide an explanatory metaphor for the dreamer's emotional state.)

Hoss, Robert J. **Dream Language: Self-Understanding through Imagery and Color.** Ashland, OR: Innersource, 2005. (Explores dream language in terms of the newest information on the dreaming brain. Pioneering work with color in dreams. Excellent process for dialoguing with dream symbols. Regular updates appear on his website, www.dreamscience.org.)

Johnson, Robert A. **Inner Work: Using Dreams and Active Imagination for Personal Growth**. HarperSanFrancisco, 1986. (A classic in dream work and active imagination.)

Jung, C.G. **Memories, Dreams, Reflections**. New York: Random House, 1962. (Jung's autobiographical journey into healing including his own major dreams.)

Krakow, Barry. **Turning Nightmares into Dreams** (Re-scripting process) The book and CDs are available from http://www.nightmaretreatment.com.

Lasley, Justina. **Honoring the Dream: A Handbook for Dream Group Leaders**. Mount Pleasant, SC, 2004. (An essential resource for dream-group facilitators.) May be ordered from http://www.dreamsynergy.org/honoringthedream.htm

Newman, Zoe. **Lucid Waking: Using Dreamwork Principles to Transform Your Everyday Life.** Berkeley, CA: White Egret Press, 2010. (This book provides many exercises for participants in the IASD Cancer Project.)

Norment, Rachel. **Guided by Dreams: Breast Cancer, Dreams, and Transformation.** Richmond: Brandylane Pubishers, 2006. (Dreams, art work, and the journey into healing of a breast cancer survivor.)

Sanford, John A. **Dreams and Healing: A Succinct and Lively Interpretation of Dreams**. New York: Paulist Press, 1978. (Wonderful examples of evolution of positive imagery matching growth of positive emotions through several series of dreams.)

Siegel, Alan and Kelly Bulkeley. **Dreamcatching: Every Parent's Guide to Exploring and Understanding Children's Dreams and Nightmares**. New York: Three Rivers Press, 1998.

Taylor, Jeremy. **The Living Labyrinth: Exploring Universal Themes in Myths, Dreams, and the Symbolism of Everyday Life**. Mahwah, NJ: Paulist Press, 1998. (Exploring universal themes)

Taylor, Jeremy. **The Wisdom of Your Dreams**. New York: Tarcher/ Penguin, 2009. (Expanded edition of original classic with new data on dreams and the evolution of consciousness. Includes guidelines for dream groups.)

Ullman, Montague and Nan Zimmerman. **Working with Dreams**. New York:Harper Collins, 1989. (Group dream sharing approach with emphasis on discovery and safety of the dreamer.)

Van de Castle, Robert L. **Our Dreaming Mind**. New York: Ballentine Books,1994. (History and scope of the entire field of dreaming. Includes chapters on somatic contributions to dreams.)

GUIDED IMAGERY

Naparstek, Belleruth. **Staying Well with Guided Imagery.** Time Warner Books, 1994. (Classic book on Guided Imagery for healthcare settings. Excellent scripts. Adaptable for use with dream imagery.)

Naparstek**. Invisible Heroes: Survivors of Trauma and How They Heal.** New York: Bantam Books, 2006. ((Nightmare approaches with Post tramatic-stress survivors. Excellent summaries of PTS research.)

Davenport, Leslie. **Healing and Transformation through Guided Imagery**. Berkeley, CA: Celestial Arts, 2009. (Very spiritual approach to Guided Imagery.)

Samuels, Michael, M.D. **Healing with the Mind's Eye**. Hoboken, NJ: Wiley, 1990. (Wisdom from an early pioneer in using imagery in healthcare settings.)

Rossman, Martin L., M.D. **Guided Imagery for Self-Healing**. New World Library, 2000 . (Another classic. Scripts for dialoguing with an Inner Healer, symptoms, and resistance. Adaptable for use with dream imagery.)

Rossman. **Fighting Cancer from Within**, New York: Henry Holt & Company, 2003. (Excellent scripts for stimulating the immune system, undergoing treatment and surgery, and dealing with side effects.)

Simonton, O. Carl, M.D. and Stephanie Mathews Simonton and James L. Creighton. **Getting Well Again**. New York: Bantam Books, 1992. (Reissue of a classic that first brought attention to use of guided imagery with cancer patients.)

INTEGRATIVE ONCOLOGY

Abrams, Donald, M.D. and Weil, Andrew, M.D., eds. **Integrative Oncology.** Oxford University Press, 2009. (Collection of mind/body research relevant to cancer patients. Research on meditation, imagery, expressive arts, and energy applicable to a meditative dream-work approach.)

Geffen, Jeremy, M.D. **The Journey Through Cancer: Healing and Transforming the Whole Person**. New York: Three Rivers Press, 2000 and 2006. (A strong advocate for integrating mind, body, and spirit.)

Learner, Michael. **Choices in Healing,: Integrating the Best of Conventional and Complementary Approaches to Cancer**. Cambridge, MA: MIT Press, 1994. (Conventional and complementary approaches for cancer. Research on meditation, imagery, expressive arts, and energy applicable to a meditative dream work approach.)

Mumber, Matthew P., M.D., ed. **Integrative Oncology: Principles and Practice**, London and New York: Taylor & Francis, 2006. (Research on meditation, imagery, expressive arts and energy applicable to a meditative dream work approach.)

Simon, David, M.D. **Return to Wellness: Embracing Body, Mind, and Spirit in the Face of Cancer.** New York: Wiley, 1999. (Many practical exercises)

MIND-BODY MEDICINE

Benson, Herbert, M.D. **The Relaxation Response**. New York: Harper Torch, 1975. (The physiological benefits of relaxation underlie every meditation approach. Research applicable to a meditative dream work approach.)

Barasch, Marc Ian. **The Healing Path**. New York: Putnam, 1992. (Examples and reflections on contributing factors in cases of spontaneous remission.)

Doidge, Norman, M.D. **The Brain that Changes Itself**. New York: Penguin Books, 2007. (Chapters on imagination and psychoanalysis show the power of dreams and dream work to change the brain.)

Dossey, Larry. **Reinventing Medicine: Beyond Mind-Body to a New Era of Healing**. New York: Harper Collins, 1999. (Conventional medicine must address mind and spirit as well as body; must deal with meaning.)

Kabat-Zinn, Jon. **Full Catastrophe Living: Using the Wisdom of Your Body and Mind to Face Stress, Pain, and Illness**. New York: Dell Publishing, 1990. (The Program of the Stress Reduction Clinic at the University of Massachusetts Medical Center.)

Le Shan, Lawrance. **Cancer as a Turning Point: A Handbook for People with Cancer, Their Families and Health Professionals**. New York: Penguin Books, 1994. (Classic by a pioneer mind-body psychotherapist showing that living a fuller life is the key to enhancing the immune system.)

Pert, Candace B. **Molecules of Emotion.** New York, Simon and Schuster, 1999. (Explains the biochemical links between mind and body; emotions and immunology are interdependent. Emphasizes the importance of finding creative expression for all emotions. Pert works conscientiously with her own dreams.)

Remen, Rachel Naomi, M.D. **My Grandfather's Blessings: Stories of Strength, Refuge, and Belonging**. New York: Riverhead Books, 2000. (Inspiration from the "Mother" of mind-body-spirit medicine.)

Rosen, David H., M.D. **Transforming Depression: Healing the Soul through Creativity**, 2002. (Jungian psychiatrist advocates mind/body approaches.)

Siegel, Bernard, M.D. **Love, Medicine and Miracles**. New York: Harper & Row, 1986. (An inspiration and guide for becoming an "exceptional" cancer patient.)

WEBSITES

The International Association for the Study of Dreams (IASD): www.asdreams.org

IASD Cancer Project: www.healingpowerofdreams.com

Belleruth Naparstek: www.healthjourneys.com

Rossman, Martin L. M.D.: www.thehealingmind.org

Jeremy Taylor: www.jeremytaylor.com

Robert Hoss: www.dreamscience.org

Patricia Garfield: www.creativeliving.org

Justina Lasley: www.dreamsynergy.org

Ernest Hartmann, M.D. web.me.com/ernesthartmann

The Haden Institute: www.hadeninstitute.com

Sheila Asato: www.monkeybridgearts.com

Barry Krakow: www.nightmaretreatment.com.

All Things Healing, Dream Medicine Page: www.allthingshealing.com

END NOTES

CHAPTER 1

(1)   The opening ritual is at the discretion of the facilitator. Some prefer a few moments of silence. The key is to allow the group to move into a deeper meditative space.

(2)   Ullman-Taylor Group Projective Approach: Montague Ullman developed a dream-group sharing approach emphasizing safety of the dreamer and discovery. Grounded in Ullman's work, Jeremy Taylor has individualized and expanded the projective method for group dream-sharing in every kind of setting all over the world.
Montague Ullman and Nan Zimmerman. *Working With Dreams*. New York: Dellacorte, 1979.
Jeremy Taylor. *Dream Work: Techniques for Discovering the Creative Power in Dreams*. New York: Paulist Press, 1983.

(3)   Clarifying questions are part of the process as practiced in the IASD Cancer Project. See Appendix I.

(4)   IASD Ethics Statement is adhered to by all IASD Cancer Project facilitators. See Appendix II.

(5)   Discussion of the projection process as practiced in the IASD Cancer Project is in Appendix I.

CHAPTER 2
(1)   Pioneering research: Herbert Benson. *The Relaxation Response.* New York: Harper Torch, 1975.

(2)   Edmund Jacobsen in the 1930's was a pioneer in muscle physiology. Simplified versions of his progressive muscular relaxation technique are commonly used in many meditative practices.

CHAPTER 3
(1)   Robert J. Hoss. *Dream Language: Self Understanding through Imagery and Color.* Ashland, OR: Innersource, 2005, 36-49.

(2)   Hoss, 36-53.

(3)   Hoss, 151-184.

(4)   Norman Doidge. *The Brain that Changes Itself.* New York: Penguin, 2007. 215-244.

(5)   Jeremy Taylor. *The Living Labyrinth: Exploring Universal Themes in Myths, Dreams, and the Symbolism of Everyday Life.* Mahwah, NJ: Paulist Press, 1998.
Patricia Garfield in *The Universal Dream Key.* Harper SanFrancisco, 2001, provides a classic on universal dream themes.

CHAPTER 4
(1)   Many sources discuss how dreams may alert us to disturbed physiological functioning:
Robert L. Van de Castle. *Our Dreaming Mind.* New York: Ballantine, 1994, 361-370 (highlights the research of Russian psychiatrist Vasily Kasakin and sites other leading proponents of diagnostic dreams).

Patricia Garfield. *The Healing Power of Dreams*. New York: Simon and Schuster, 1991 (speaks of dreams that predict illness).

Jeremy Taylor describes a dream very similar to Margaret's that alerted the dreamer to ovarian cancer. Taylor says, "There is . . . an aspect of every dream that provides an exquisitely accurate 'readout' of your physical health and condition of your body at the moment of the dream." *The Wisdom of Your Dreams*. New York: Tarcher/Penguin, 2009, 10-17.

(2)   Similar dreams are recorded by Marc Ian Barasch. *Healing Dreams*. New York, Riverhead Books, 2000. He recounts his journey through thyroid cancer.

(3)   Ernest Hartmann, *Dreams and Nightmares*. New York: Perseus Book Group, 2001. Updates appear regularly on his website, web. me.com/ernesthartmann

(4)   Hoss, 3-11.

(5)   Candace B. Pert, *Molecules of Emotions: The Science Behind Mind-Body Medicine*. New York: Simon and Schuster, New York, 1997, 290-292.

(6)   Doidge, 230-244.

(7)   There are many symbol dictionaries. Two that Dream Circle members sometimes find useful are *An Illustrated Encyclopedia for Traditional Symbols*, J.C. Cooper, ed. London: Thames and Hudson, Ltd., 1978 and Sandra A. Thomson. *Cloud Nine: A Dreamer's Dictionary*. New York: Avon Books, 1994.

(8)   Classics in the field of guided imagery for healthcare are Belleruth Naparstek. *Staying Well With Guided Imagery*. New York, Warner, 1994; Martin L. Rossman, *Guided Imagery for Self-Healing*. New World Library, 2000; and Martin L. Rossman, *Fighting Cancer from Within: How to Use the Power of Your Mind for Healing*. New York: Henry Holt, 2003.

(9)   At www.healthjourneys.com, type *Archives* in the search box. When it opens, click *Solutions and Support* at the top of the page. From *Topics* on the left hand side, choose *Cancer/ Oncology*. Research summaries are interspersed among case studies.

(10)   *Integrative Oncology, Principles and Practice*, compiled and edited by Matthew P. Mumber. London and New York: Taylor and Francis, 2006.
Integrative Oncology, compiled and edited by Donald Abrams and Andrew Weil. London: Oxford U.P., 2009.

(11)   Belleruth Naparstek. *Invisible Heroes: Survivors of Trauma and How They Heal*. New York: Bantam Books, 2006.

(12)   www.healingpowerofdreams.com

(13)   Stephen LaBerge and Howard Reingold. *Exploring the World of Lucid Dreaming*. New York: Ballentine, 1990.
Ryan Hurd. *Lucid Immersion Guidebook: A Holistic Blueprint for Lucid Dreaming*. Philadelphia: Dream Studies Press, 2012.
Robert Waggoner. *Lucid Dreaming: Gateway to the Inner Self*. Needham, MA: Moment Point 2009.

(14)   Barry Krakow, www.nightmaretreatment.com

(15)   This advice comes from Beverly Donavan. Her work with veterans suffering post-traumatic stress is described by Naparstek in *Invisible Heroes*, 181-182, 308-311, 324, 338-339.

(16)   Alan Siegel and Kelley Bulkeley. *Dreamcatching: Every Parent's Guide to Exploring and Understanding Children's Dreams and Nightmares*. New York: Three Rivers Press, 1998.
Ann Sayre Wiseman. *Nightmare Help: A Guide for Parents and Teachers*. Berkeley: Ten Speed, 1989.

CHAPTER 5

(1)   Jungian analyst Jutta von Buchholtz kindly discussed with the author her analogy of the shadow falling from the tree onto the child, 2/16/12.

(2)   Appendix I. Dream Group Guidelines

(3)   Jutta von Buchholtz, telephone conversation, 2/16/12

(4)   Definition of the Self is found in C.G. Jung, ed. *Man and His Symbols*. New York: Dell, 1964, 163.

(5)   A classic book on Shadow: Robert A. Johnson. *Owning Your Own Shadow* . HarperSanFrancisco, 1991.

(6)   Dream Circle members are particularly fond of Ted Andrews' *Animal Speak*. St. Paul, 2001.

(7)   Discussion of anima/animus is found in C.G. Jung, *Collective Works*, Vol.9, Part 1, 2nd ed., (Princeton U. P., 1968) par. 451.

(8)   James Hollis. *The Eden Project: In Search of the Magical Other.* ON, Canada: Inner City Books, 1998).
John Sanford. *Invisible Partners.* Mahwah, N.J.: Paulist Press,1980.

CHAPTER 6

(1)   Hoss, 145. Worksheet 2 in the back of the book will give you the opportunity to repeat the exercise as many times as you choose.

(2)   Michael Lerner quotes Rachel Naomi Remen in *Choices in Healing: Integrating the Best of Conventional and Complementary Approaches to Cancer.* Cambridge: MIT Press, 1999, 124-125.

(3)   C.G. Jung speaks of the Self as appearing in dreams as a "superordinate" personality in "Definitions," the Collective Works 6, par. 790.

(4)   Robert A. Johnson. *Inner Work: Using Dreams and Active Imagination for Personal Growth.* HarperSanFrancisco, 1986, 197-199.

(5)   Rossman offers a script for listening to your symptoms *in Guided Imagery for Self-Healing,* 132-135.

CHAPTER 7

(1)   C.G. Jung wrote about the "numinous" experience in his the first volume of *Jung's Letters,* Gerhard Adler and Aniela Jaffe, editors (Princeton University Press, 1973). Also in "Psychology and Religion," Collective Works 11, par. 6.

(2)   Studies confirming rapid healing with imagery are found in Mumber (2006) and Abrams and Weil, (2009).

(3)   Rossman writes about depression in *Fighting Cancer from Within*, 28-29.

(4)   Taylor, *The Wisdom Of Your Dreams*, 265.

(5)   Barasch, *Healing Dreams*.
Wanda Easter Burch. *She Who Dreams*. Novata, CA.: New World Library, 2003.
Rachel Norment. *Guided by Dreams: Breast Cancer, Dreams, and Transformation*, Richmond: Brandylane Publishers, 2006.

(6)   At www.healthjourneys.com, type *Archives* in the search box. When it opens, click *Solutions and Support* at the top of the page. From Topics on the left hand side, choose Cancer/Oncology. Re-search summaries are interspersed among case studies.

(7)   Garfield, *The Healing Power of Dreams*.

(8)   Hoss, *Dream Language*, 21.

(9)   Kelly Bulkeley. *Dreams of Healing: Transforming Nightmares into Visions of Hope*. Mahwah, N.J., Paulist Press, 2003.

(10)   The QOL surveys with ongoing cancer groups have been taken with an unstandardized instrument. The IASD Cancer Project will begin using a standardized instrument in 2012.

(11)   Spontaneous remission is discussed in Mark Barasch. *The Healing Path: A Soul Approach to Illness*. New York. Tarcher /Putnam, 1993.
Andrew Weil. *Spontaneous Healing*. New York: Random House, 1995.

(12)   Martin Rossman. *Guided Imagery for Self-Healing.* New World Library, 2000, 199.

CHAPTER 8
(1)   Taylor, *The Wisdom Of Your Dreams,* 164.

(2)   Kelley Bulkeley and Patricia Bulkley. *Dreaming Beyond Death.* Boston: Beacon Press, 2005.
Nicole Gratton and Monique Sequin. *The Benefits of Dreams Before, During, and After Death.* (to be published in 2012.)
Patricia Garfield. *Dream Messenger: How Dreams of the Departed Bring Healing Gifts* .New York, Simon and Schuster, 1997.

CHAPTER 9
(1)   Carl Gustav Jung, *Synchronicity: An Acausal Connecting Principle,* trans. R.F.C. Hall,
Princeton, N.J.: Princeton U.P., Bollingen Series,1973. This is the first Princeton/ Bollingen paperback edition. Reissued with a new forward by Sonu Shamdasani in 2010.

(2)   Robert J. Hoss comments that many people attribute déjà vu experiences to precognitive dreams. He also speaks of an alternative theory based on sensory events being processed by two paths to the brain. "Sensory information takes a fast track to the limbic system where emotions and emotional memories are associated with the sensory event in order to prepare us for action. The slower track goes to the cognitive centers where the event, plus the emotional information, raises our attention level so that we become aware of it. It is reasonable that the perception of an event, together with a construct of similar emotional memories, could produce a feeling of having been there before." *Dream Language,* 27.

(3)   We refer readers who are interested in the wisdom of the body to the writings of Arnold Mindell, Louise Hay, Caroline Myss, and Mona Lisa Schultz.

(4)   A clear and easy-to-use translation is by Brian Browne Walker. *The I Ching or Book of Changes* (New York: St. Martin's Griffin, 1992.

(5)   Zoe Newman. *Lucid Waking: Using the Dreamwork Principles to Transform Your Everyday Life*. Berkeley, White Egret Press, 2010.

(6)   Newman, 54.

(7)   Naparstek, *Staying Well With Guided Imagery*.
Rossman, *Fighting Cancer from Within*.
Rossman, *Guided Imagery for Self-Healing*.

CHAPTER 10

(1)   Studies showing the positive effects of expressive art can be found in Mumber (2006) and Abrams and Weil (2009).

(2)   Studies showing the positive effects of meditative movement can be found in Mumber (2006) and Abrams and Weil, (2009).

(3)   Naparstek, *Staying Well With Guided Imagery*, 62.

(4)   Studies showing the success of guided imagery for controlling pain can be found in Mumber (2006) and Abrams and Weil (2009).

(5)   Studies showing the value of using guided imagery both before and after surgery can be found in Mumber (2006) and Abrams and Weil (2009).

(6)   Blue Shield report to National Managed Health Care Congress, Baltimore, MD., 2002.

(7)   The use of ritual to integrate healing imagery: Jeanne Achterberg, Barbara Dossey, and Leslie Kolkmeier: *Rituals of Healing*. New York: Random House, 1994.
Johnson, *Inner Work*, 97-134, 196-199.

(8)   The rediscovery of the importance of dreams in the institutional church and guides with which to work with one's own dreams: John A. Sandford. *Dreams: God's Forgotten Language*. HarperSanFrancisco, 1968 and 1989; Joyce Rockwood Hudson. *Natural Spirituality: Recovering the Wisdom Tradition in Christianity*. JRH Publications, 2000; Robert L. Haden. *Unopened Letters from God*. (Haden Institute Publishing, 2010); Tallulah Lyons. *Dream Prayers: Dreamwork as a Spiritual Path*. Smyrna, GA: Tallulah Lyons Publisher, 2000.

(9)   Jon Kabat-Zinn. *Coming to Our Senses: Healing Ourselves and the World Through Mindfulness*. New York: Hyperion, 2005.

CHAPTER 11

(1)   The CA 125 is a biomarker that has proved useful in charting the progress of many woman undergoing already-diagnosed ovarian cancer. Computerized Axial Tomography (CAT scan), more commonly known by its abbreviated name, CT scan, combines many x-ray images with the use of a computer to generate cross-sectional, often, 3-dimensional images.

(2)   Chelsea Wakefield elaborates on this subject in *Negotiating the Inner Peace Treaty*. Bloomington, IN: Balboa, 2012.

(3)   Andreas Mavromatis. *Hypnogogia: The Unique State of Consciousness between Wakefulness and Sleep*. London: Thyrsos, 3rd. ed., 2010.

(4)   David Servan-Schreiber, *Anticancer: A New Way of Life*. New York: Penguin, 2008.

(5)   Servan-Schreiber.

(6)   Joseph Campbell. *The Hero with a Thousand Faces*. Princeton, NJ: Princeton U. P., 1973.
The hero's journey through healing is told by Barasch in *The Healing Path*.

(7) Summary of research on humor: Hunaid Hasan and Fatema Hasan: "Laugh Yourself into a Healthier Person: A Cross Cultural Analysis of the Effects of Laughter on Health," International Journal of Medical Sciences, 2009; 6(4)200-211. Available from www.medsci.org/v060200.htm.

(8)   Positive effects of imagery for cancer patients can be found in Rossman, *Fighting Cancer from Within*.
At www.healthjourneys.com, type *Archives* in the search box. When it opens, click *Solutions and Support* at the top of the page. When you see *Topics* on the left hand side, choose *Cancer/Oncology*. Research summaries are interspersed among case studies.

(9)   Hartmann, *Dreams and Nightmares*. Hartmann's research with thousands of dreams shows that the central imagery of the dream reflects the dreamer's primary emotional concern.

About the Author

Tallulah Lyons, M.Ed., has always loved her dreams and has expressed them in paint and clay since she was a little girl. She majored in English Literature in college, and then became a special education teacher and consultant for many years. During this career, she found dreams and guided imagery to be a natural road into the heart of almost any child. Tallulah became a certified dream facilitator at the Haden Institute and is currently on the faculty of the Haden Summer Conference. She has been facilitating dream appreciation and guided imagery with cancer survivors and their caregivers for fifteen years. She is on the staff of two cancer wellness facilities in Atlanta, GA, and is the co-creator of the International Association for the Study of Dreams (IASD) Cancer Project. Her hope is that the project will continue to develop and expand.

Tallulah lives with her husband in Atlanta. She has two grown children and five grandchildren. She cares very deeply about dream work as a spiritual practice and is the author of *Dream Prayers, Dreamwork as a Spiritual Path*. Tallulah is available for workshops and presentations. You may contact her at www.healingpowerofdreams.com